Get A Raise in 60 Days

Get a
Raise
in
60
Days

Para Research
Rockport
Massachusetts

Get A Raise in 60 Days
by Steve Kravette

Library of Congress Catalog Card Number: 83-060061
International Standard Book Number: 0-914918-46-X

Type set in 10½ pt. Paladium on a Compugraphic 8400
Cover design by Ralph Poness
Cover illustration by Joe Veno
Typesetting by Sinikka Nogelo
Edited by Shaun Levesque and Marah Ren

Printed by R.R. Donnelley & Sons Co.
on 55-pound Cream White paper

Published by Para Research, Inc.
Gloucester, Massachusetts 01930

Manufactured in the United States of America

First Printing, June 1983,. 10,000 copies

Dedication

With Love to Jan.
This is it.
That's all there is to it.

Contents

1

The Way It Is

No one succeeds in business without really trying. Good luck won't do it anymore. Neither will good looks. You can't sit back and wait for success to come to you.

Everyone who talks about today's economic scene paints a picture in dark, murky, overcast colors. And when economists, the federal government and national surveys say things will be bad on a large scale it can easily be interpreted to mean things will be bad for you because:

In the first place, there aren't enough jobs to go around these days.

And in the second, if you are lucky enough to find a job, there aren't enough promotions or raises available these days. The corporate and job advancement ladders are as conjested as the unemployment lines. So not only isn't there a fast way up, sometimes there isn't even a slow way.

The shortage of jobs at every level of the company structure means that people just don't move up through the ranks the way they used to. Raises don't add up the way you'd like them to anymore. And, inflation takes an ever-increasing bite out of our wallet.

Finally, the word is that this condition is not likely to change. It is expected to keep on getting worse.

When I wrote *Get A Job in 60 Seconds*, I knew what the experts had to say about the scarcity of jobs. I didn't buy it. So I presented a system for getting the job you want anyway.

The book wasn't about proving the experts wrong or demonstrating that what they're saying isn't so. The book was about how you, as a powerful and creative individual, can override negative statistics, cruise right over obstacles and predictions of gloom and doom, and win in low-win or even no-win situations.

When I wrote *Get A Job in 60 Seconds*, I didn't know what the experts had to say about the scarcity of raises and advancement opportunities.

So this book is to complete both the job started in that book and the job you may have started using that book.

Of course, this book will help you whether or not you have read my last book. Or anybody else's book for that matter. It can help you win at the job you've had all along.

And the way you'll win is to get more money in less time. Or a raise in 60 days.

Why 60 days?

Because if you are willing to align yourself with this book and follow the suggestions outlined for you, 60 days is all you will need.

Perhaps you can get your raise even sooner. If you are a truly powerful communicator, it may take only 60 minutes for your boss to see your value to the company and reward you appropriately. However, it usually takes approximately a month to undercut impressions people at work have already formed about you. It then takes approximately another month to lock new and more positive evaluations and judgments in place.

By the time your supervisor begins to think, "Wow, Susan used to be the laziest person I ever saw and now she's sparkplugging the whole department," your raise will be around the corner.

To get your raise in 60 days you need to start at the beginning. And the very first thing to get clear about is who you are. You are you. Whatever your name is. If you have any question about that, get up right now and check yourself out in the nearest mirror.

Now that's settled.

So I don't need to tell you who you are anymore. Instead, I'll tell you what you're not. Just once. And just for the record. What you are not is a statistic or a number or any part of anyone else's cumulative data.

That means whatever is true for statistics and other forms of databases, and all the people who are willing to be included in them, does not necessarily have to be true for you. Because you're not any of that.

Once you are not willing to be lumped with everyone else, or to be just a small part of a large trend, it all gets easier. More or less.

There's still something important to clean up. And that's what getting a raise looks like to you.

Getting a raise probably looks hard. It looks risky. It looks as if you will have to confront someone.

Almost everyone is uncomfortable about asking for a raise and about handling the feelings of vulnerability and fear of rejection that go along with asking.

The way you've been going about it so far, there's no way around that. It's the truth. Asking for a raise is definitely hard. And risky. It may mean a confrontation. And all the rest.

Asking for a raise also has had a funny way of *not* working about as often as it works. So far. It's been truly difficult.

Picture how it looks for just a moment.

You screw down your shaky courage and you go in to see the boss. Your heart is pounding in your chest. Your stomach is all knotted up. Your throat and shoulders are tight. You're hardly breathing at all. And your voice is tiny and sticks in your dry throat.

Will you ever get a raise by asking for it that way? Maybe not. It is certainly a hard way to do it.

Hoping for a raise is even harder. You just stick around, show up every day and wait for the next review or the next fiscal year or the next big contract, and you hope.

When one of those things happens, maybe you'll get your raise. Or maybe you'll get canned instead. More likely they'll just forget about you all together. All you have been doing is not calling attention to yourself. And that's what happens. No one pays any attention to you. If asking for a raise is a fifty-fifty proposition, the success rate of hoping for a raise is less than one in a hundred.

Even lower on the scale of probable success are demanding a raise, pleading for a raise and doing anything that quickly comes to mind about getting someone to give you a raise.

The big mistake in each of these good-old-traditional-raise-getting techniques is the same. And it is the major source of the problems that keep your paycheck from growing.

Why should your boss give you a raise for sitting around hoping, wishing or praying when he or she can just go out and hire someone else for less? Unemployment is predicted to remain high during the next few years. There are lots of people who could do your job and many of them are available for work right this minute.

I'll tell you how to leap over traditional techniques and problems and how to get your raise in Chapter 10. But first, there's a lot you may need to discover about yourself and your work.

Until now, your whole approach has been wrong. On several counts.

First, you have probably always thought you weren't making enough money. And that not making or having enough money were reasons enough to get your boss to give you more.

No way.

You'll get to look at money at length in Chapter 4, and you'll see how you can begin to always have enough of it. Remember, no one will ever give you a raise to reduce your hardships or balance the injustices of the world.

Second, you've probably thought you deserved a raise. You probably thought that the length of time since your last raise or the way you put up with all the aggravating working conditions gives you some kind of divine right to more money after a while.

Guess again. Hardly anyone will ever give you a raise for reasons like those. Reasons like those have no impact. They carry no clout. They do not make any difference at all. Not ever.

Reasons such as those may get you an increase in salary. An increase is a lot less money than a raise. You get an increase for waiting around long enough or because everyone else got one too. If you're reading this book, you're playing for higher stakes than that.

Third and most important of all, no matter what else you thought, you have probably always believed that getting a raise involved somebody else giving you one and that someone else was in control of the process. So naturally, you had to ask, prove yourself, manipulate circumstances or otherwise get someone else to do something about your need or desire for more money.

Wrong again.

That one mistake has kept more people earning less money than anything else.

To get a raise in 60 days, begin by cancelling that belief, erasing it, dissolving it or doing anything it takes to eradicate it.

Instead, hold on to this: Getting a raise in 60 days simply involves getting a raise in 60 days.

It does not involve getting your boss to give you a raise. Even though that's exactly what your boss will ultimately do.

As long as you delegate the responsibility for your raise to your boss, you are at your boss's mercy. And on your boss's timetable.

When you take over complete responsibility for your raise and become the sole causal agent for creating it, getting a raise in 60 days begins to look very easy.

No matter how impossible that may sound right now, stick around.

By the time you finish this book, you will be in complete touch with your own power to create what you want for yourself. You'll do it without buying in to trends, statistics, performance standards or other people's considerations of any kind.

You will see how it works when you begin to cause the events you want in your life, instead of just waiting or hoping for them to happen. And those events will include financial abundance.

As part of the payoff, this book will arm you with a system for getting the raise you want.

Based upon interviews with a wide variety of executives, managers, supervisors and other people powerful enough to increase their employees' paychecks, this system will work for you. It will work simply by showing you how to take over and begin to produce results that produce raises.

What's so nice about all this is, it doesn't matter what your job is or how long you have been working at it or what traditional salary review procedures are in effect.

If there is any way in the universe to shake a raise down from your employer's money tree, and you can bet that there is, this book will tell you how to do it and support you all along the way. That will start the process of you supporting yourself in the style to which you would like to become accustomed.

In just 60 days.

HOW TO GET MORE MONEY

- Remember that you are you. You are not a statistic.
- Don't try to get a raise just because you need more money or deserve more money.
- Realize that you create your raise. No one gives it to you.

2
Tight Money and All That Stuff

Did you ever wonder what was really going on at work that made big fat raises so hard to get?

Money at work is probably so tight because so many people at work are tight. And I don't mean stingy. I mean tense.

A tight presentation, style or way of being freezes out raises completely. On the other hand, no matter how tight the economy is, it has never stopped anyone who should get a raise from getting a raise. It only stops people who should not get raises from getting a raise.

Remember that the next time you hear a tight person talking about tight money and hard times being the reasons why raises are scarce.

So what is it that actually makes raises scarce if it's not the economy?

A lot of stuff.

Picture this:

Every morning, everywhere, millions and millions of people get up, go to the bathroom, brush their teeth, get dressed and go to work.

Some of them drive. Some walk. Some take a subway, a bus, a plane, a cab, a bike.

Some of these millions and millions of people go to work in factories. Some in offices. Some in stores. Still others in hospitals, forests, balloons, hamburger stands and homes.

Just like you.

And just like you, nobody goes to work alone. Even if you go to work by yourself with no carpoolers, no other public transportation riders and no friends, you don't go to work alone.

Even if you go to work in a private car or a private jet, or with a private paper bag over your head, you don't go to work alone.

You always take your stuff with you. You take years and years and piles and piles and stacks and stacks of stuff.

Some of the stuff you take along is your body and all its sensations. You feel achy or tired. Your muscles hurt from too much jogging or too much lying around. You may have a cold, a headache, a toothache or a bunyon.

Physical sensations and symptoms are part of the stuff you always bring with you. And, chances are, you think that physical stuff means something. So you probably act tired or sluggish or just generally low-key.

Some of the stuff you take along is your emotion of the moment. You feel angry or sad or depressed or bored or apathetic or wonderful or highly enthusiastic. You always feel something, even when you don't acknowledge what the emotion that you feel is. And you always bring that feeling with you.

Once again, you probably think that emotional stuff means something. So you may act withdrawn, nasty, loud, quiet or whatever you are feeling.

Some of the stuff you take along every day when you go to work is your thoughts. You hear a little voice in the middle of your head and it tells you things like this: "It's too nice a day to go to work." And "I wonder how I'll ever make my next car payment." And "That woman looks like Sophia Loren." And "That man is walking as though he's drunk." And "Oh God, I'm going to be late again."

Hundreds of thoughts like those go everywhere that you go.

Because you usually think that your thoughts have meaning, you generally manage to act them out in some way.

The other stuff you take to work with you is your attitudes, positions, considerations and beliefs. You stand firmly planted on a platform of premises. Like: Work stinks. Age and treachery will always win over youth and trust. Times are hard right now and money is tight. Life is tough. Just one more degree will get me a promotion. No matter how hard I try, I will never get anywhere around here. Someday I'll be happy.

All your attitudes, positions, considerations and beliefs tag along with you every morning. And that's not all.

Still more of your stuff includes everything other people have ever told you. You can probably hear the voice and see the face of the person who said: "July will be cold and rainy this year." And "Mr. Bigdome is going to retire in six months." And "The plant's closing down and we're all gonna get laid off." And "Russia is about to bomb us so nothing matters anyway."

Everything everybody ever told you also goes with you.

That's almost all of it.

Last, but nowhere near least, the stuff you carry to work with you every morning includes all your images and pictures from the past. The time the cute redheaded boy laughed at you at the school dance. The time your best friend let you down. The time you lied on your expense account. The time you cheated on your husband or wife. The time you didn't get a raise or a promotion. Every time you felt embarrassed or humiliated. Everything you remember about growing up. And everything you think you don't. All those pictures and images from your past.

It's all part of your stuff.

And you take your stuff very seriously. So you take it, all of it, everywhere you go. That includes packing it all off to work with you every morning.

Like your physical sensations, your emotions, and your thoughts, you think all of it means something. And that all of it is important. So you find lots and lots of ways to add all of it, piece by piece and trickle by trickle, to whatever you do at work.

Given all that, is it any wonder that some days your life seems loaded down beyond belief?

And that you don't have enough energy to do the things you want to do?

And that your job doesn't seem to go as well as you'd like?

And that you don't feel as if you are getting the salary you need to survive?

It is no wonder at all.

Considering all your stuff and the way you use it, everything you've just read would have to be the way it is for you.

That's the bad news.

The good news is, from now on all that does not need to ever be the same again. All those memories, sensations and the rest of it are just stuff. Stuff is the best thing to call it because that's all it is. It just drags you down.

This book is going to empower you to clear it all up. And to keep it clear. For as long as you want.

Until now, part of the problem has been that you probably didn't know just how many tons and tons of stuff you have been carrying around with you and taking to work with you each day.

A funny thing about stuff. When you don't know you've got it and you don't know what the content of it is, it runs you. It dominates your whole life.

Literally.

Your body sensations, emotions, thoughts, attitudes, positions, considerations, beliefs, accumulated truths from outside sources and past pictures team up to keep you from doing your job.

All that stuff also keeps you from clearly focusing on what you want and intend to have in life. It creates conflicting desires and beliefs. It limits your capacity to see yourself as you really are and your field of experience as it really is.

Because of that, you keep giving in to the circumstances of your life. And whether you feel hopeless about them or optimistic about your capacity to change them, you have been living and working without activating an incredibly powerful connection with the part of yourself that invariably produces results.

Here's a perfect example.

You have a job. And you are at a point where your salary doesn't cover your expenses anymore. So you're unhappy about that. (Emotional stuff.) Maybe you're angry about that too. (More emotional stuff.)

You think a nice fat raise would solve everything. (Thought stuff.) But you just read in the papers that a recession is here, money is scarce, many wages are frozen. (Stuff someone else told you.) Your friend Hilda calls up and tells you she just asked her boss for a raise and got fired instead. (More stuff someone else told you.) You get upset. (Emotional stuff.) And you get a little scared. (More emotional stuff.)

You get the idea that you are stuck. (Attitude stuff.) It begins to look hopeless. (Positional stuff.) And you believe that in times like these, we all have to sit tight, pull in our belts, pitch in and shut up. (Belief system stuff.)

Lately, when you go to work, you notice you have headaches. (Body sensation stuff.) Or maybe stomach aches. (More body sensation stuff.) And that you've been catching a lot of colds this year. (More body sensation stuff.) All that begins to worry you. (Emotional and thought stuff.)

You remember how hard your parents had to work for a living, how tired they always were at night. (Picture stuff from the past.) You also remember times you asked for raises and got turned down. (More stuff from past pictures.)

You think you don't know what to do. (Thought stuff.) And you think that your boss is a cheap, mean SOB. (More thought stuff.)

And on and on and on.

All of that is part of the stuff you take to work with you. And it's a major contributing factor to why things just haven't been going so well lately.

What's really interesting though is now that you know all that, you don't have to change any of it. Don't even try.

No matter what, you will have all the same body sensations, feelings, thoughts, beliefs, attitudes, considerations, advice from experts and past pictures.

All of it can stay just the same as it is.

The difference is now you'll begin to know what it is when it comes up. Then you can simply include it in your life. Let it be there. Just like your pencil, your suit or the telephone message pad, and the smile that's pasted on the receptionist's face.

Those things are all there. And they don't run you or stand in the way of success or failure. Neither will your stuff. In fact, it will actually begin to mean less and less until it hardly means anything at all.

Once you begin to do that, you will notice an amazing quality of lightness in your life. As if all the heaviness you thought was a normal condition of your day-to-day existence suddenly went south and disappeared forever.

Now you can take a look at the same scene you pictured before. But in a different light.

You have your job. And you are at the point where your salary doesn't cover your expenses anymore. So you forget all the rest of it and get yourself a raise instead. Just like that.

So much for your stuff.

And now you are ready to look at the other side of the issue. What you couldn't see before, when all your stuff used to be in the way, was this:

Your boss has a whole lot of stuff too. Bosses are just like everybody else. Including you.

Every day, millions of them go to work. Just like you. And every day, all those bosses bring all their stuff to work with them. Just like you.

One of those bosses is yours.

It doesn't matter, by the way, where you work or what you do. You can be a kid with a summer job at a fast food counter or the president of a Fortune 500 corporation. You can be a machinist, a computer programmer, a migrant farmhand, a tv star, a typist, a union organizer, a mop pusher or anything in between.

If you have a job, you have a boss. And it also doesn't matter whether that boss is a man or a woman, a kid or an old-timer, a foreman, a chairman or a rich aunt. As far as this book is concerned, it's all the same. A boss is a boss.

If you have a job, there is someone who appears to control the strings of the purse that empties into your pay envelope. And that person is the one you are going to focus on. From now on.

And if that person's stuff includes a lot of thoughts, attitudes, considerations, beliefs, heresay and pictures from the past about you and the no-good way you've been handling your job, you are going to have a hard time getting your raise.

In 60 years much less 60 days.

Unless you use this book to transform all that stuff into an image of you surrounded with white-light work energy, halos and well-deserved money, you'll get absolutely nothing.

How far do you have to go to get that to happen?

It all depends. If you are at all like most people, the answer is pretty far.

Because in addition to all the stuff that looks and sounds a lot like yours, most of the bosses I surveyed for this book also have stuff standing between them and their employees' raises. Stuff like this:

"The problem around here," says the supervisor of a floor full of mid-level administrators and their support staffs at a large insurance company, "is that I feel like I'm trapped on the movie set of *9 to 5*.

"Everyone acts like they're just waiting around for lunch or coffee breaks or five o'clock. And there's an unbelievable amount of bickering, complaining, whining and competing for credit."

The head of a small finance company complains that, "All the people around here seem to be completely lifeless and bored. I don't know where they hang up their smiles when they come in, but I'd sure like to find out. It's like the cadaver room at City Hospital."

A vice-president at an electronics firm reports, "I always feel guilty when I ask anyone to do anything extra, even when something extra is an implicit part of their job, like that one final visual check of printed circuit boards before Quality Control takes over.

"And, God forbid, I should ever hear someone volunteer. For anything!

"I mean, whatever happened to just plain old-fashioned willingness to pitch in and work?"

It's interesting to notice that if your stuff includes a lot of not liking what's going on at work, your boss's stuff probably includes even more than your own. Your boss's stuff is packed with thoughts about you not liking your work and positions about you not doing your job adequately or enthusiastically enough.

And stuff like that creates more tenseness and tightness in your boss than you would ever knowingly choose for your boss to have. Tense, tight bosses are a much more real and significant barrier to getting a raise than tight money.

By now you can see that all the stuff going on between you and your boss about you and your job has just got to be looked at, accepted, acknowledged and corrected.

To get a general idea of what that means, turn to page 26. Or take out a blank piece of paper and at the top, write a heading that says "The bad things about my job are."

Now take the time to list everything you don't like about your job. From cheapness about expense reimbursement and the stuck lever on the time clock to the untidyness in the cafeteria and the single-thickness sheets of toilet paper in the bathroom.

Be really complete. Put down everything you don't like now, have not liked in the past and think you won't like in the future. A boss who picks on you. A dead end in your career. Too much seniority blocking your chances to advance. A co-worker who doesn't want to go out with you or one who does.

Put it all down. No kidding. If you are serious about getting your raise, you've got to start someplace. And this is the place.

When you are finished, turn to page 26. Or turn your paper over and write a new heading that says "The good things about my job are."

Then write down each and every good thing you can think of about your present job. Include the opportunity to advance or to learn something new. The lunch hour. Making something, selling something, creating something or serving other people in some way. Include your paycheck, small as it may be, and the attractive person down the hall. Recall everything you liked most about your job since the day you first showed up. Include it all.

List it all.

The bad things about my job are:

_____

_____

_____

_____

_____

_____

_____

_____

_____

_____

_____

The good things about my job are:

_____

_____

_____

_____

_____

_____

_____

_____

_____

_____

_____

One more exercise to go. Be sure to do this one too. It will show you exactly what is in the way of your next raise.

Use this page, or begin another blank piece of paper with a heading that says "What I think of my boss."

Start writing. List all the traits that come to mind. Include the good ones as well as the bad.

When you're finished, turn to page 28 or turn the paper over. Under a new heading that says "What my boss thinks of me," list everything about you and the way you do your job, from your boss's point of view. Tell the truth and don't leave anything out.

What I think of my boss:

_____

_____

_____

_____

_____

_____

_____

_____

_____

_____

_____

_____

_____

_____

_____

_____

What my boss thinks of me:

_____

_____

_____

_____

_____

_____

_____

_____

_____

_____

_____

_____

_____

When all four of your lists are completed, read everything back to yourself. If you are using loose papers, keep them in a special folder. You will want to refer to them later.

And don't read another word until you have done all that.

OK?

OK.

Now get ready for a big surprise. Everything you've written down so far is just more of your stuff.

None of it means anything. All of it is simply stuff you think, feel, hope, believe or have an attitude or position about.

Read it again and see for yourself. If you still don't believe it, look back at the definitions of your stuff. You'll see how all of these attitudes are the same.

None of this will help you get a raise. Even the parts you look at as being positive. Like the things you like about your job or your boss.

The reason is that none of it has anything to do with the reality of the day-by-day, moment-by-moment, experiential situation within which you can create a raise for yourself.

All of that stuff is inside of you. You carry it with you and it blocks the clarity of your vision and your natural ability to do what needs to be done.

You needed to do those lists to become fully aware of this and get the point.

The point, of course, is that getting a raise comes from something larger than your stuff. It involves operating in a wider and more expansive framework than the one you've been keeping yourself stuck in.

You will soon discover that in your wider and more expansive framework, nothing can stand in the way of your raise. Not tight money, tight bosses or any of that other stuff.

And now you are ready for the next step.

HOW TO GET MORE MONEY

- Notice that people at work are tense and tight, just like the economy.
- See how many physical sensations, preconceptions, problems and emotions go along with you to work every day and how they keep getting in your way.
- Don't try to change your stuff. Just be aware of what it does to you.
- Be aware that your boss's stuff gets in the way too.

3

The Raise Game

Just a quick summary.

Chances are, you have always thought getting a raise is hard. And you've probably thought that if you struggle through your job and don't complain too much and can wait it out until the next review, you might possibly get one. Especially since you want and need one so much.

Chances are, that's why you ended up with this book in your hands.

As you are beginning to see, this is the right book and you've had the wrong idea about raises so far.

Wanting a raise doesn't work. Needing a raise doesn't work. Hoping for a raise doesn't work. Deserving a raise doesn't work. Even thinking positively about a raise and your own self-value doesn't work. None of that works. None of it matters or has ever mattered. So for the last time, forget all that. Just let it all go.

From now on, the only thing that works and the only thing you will be doing is getting a raise. In 60 days. Or less.

Starting right here.

Did you ever notice how it's never hard to do anything you really want to do?

For instance, if you wanted to become a marathon runner, here's what you would do. You'd get out four or five days a week and run fifteen or twenty miles each day. You'd do homework by reading about what motivates successful runners and what tricks and secrets about technique or equipment cut their time. And you'd do what runners do to win. Which is, of course, to be a runner and run your butt off.

Many people who don't want to be marathon runners will tell you that's a lot of long, hard work. And if you didn't want to be a great runner, you would think so too.

But since you do want to be a great runner, the joy of running and training and conditioning is just that. A joy. It's fun. Like an invigorating game. And the better you play your running game, the more you win. And it's not so hard to play either. Simply because you want to play and because you enjoy it so much.

The same goes in most of the other areas of life.

If you wanted to have a great relationship with someone, here's what you would do. You'd get out and find a person to love. You'd look at everything you have ever done that has killed off your relationships in the past and not do that any more. For example, you would tell the truth all the time. You would never withhold what needed to be said. You'd never make your loved one wrong. And you would always support your loved one in his or her goals and opportunities to contribute to others outside of the relationship. You'd become a power source, willing and able to empower your lover's life to work. You'd do homework by reading and observing and expanding your knowledge of how other successful relationships have been sustained. And you would do what great lovers do, which is to love.

A lot of people who don't want to be in a relationship will tell you that it takes a lot of hard work to maintain one.

And if you really don't want a relationship, you would think so too.

But if you do want a great relationship, the joy of being in love and overcoming barriers to intimacy is just that. A joy. And it's fun. Like a stimulating game. And the better you play your relationship game, the more you get out of it.

Same goes across the board.

It's always the same. Training your dog to do tricks. Tap dancing. Writing a book. Inventing the next hula hoop or space invader game. Discovering a new plant. Curing an old disease. Or getting a raise.

Nothing is ever hard when producing the result is something you are really up to and fully committed to doing. Particularly when you are willing to make it fun instead of a life-and-death struggle.

In fact, much more often than not, the easiest way to get a raise in 60 days is to have so much fun doing it that your boss wants to reward you just to keep you around the place.

To do that, you have to be really clear about what your intention is. Then you have to be very clear about how you'll materialize it to get your raise. And then you have got to bring your body, your emotions, your thoughts, your pictures, your previous successes and failures and all the rest of you into a state of alignment with your intention.

Those lists in the last chapter were there so you could notice whether there was anything you needed to become aware of that might have been in the way of your raise. It would have been in the way because you didn't know it was part of the stuff you carry around with you.

There is only one thing that produces raises. And that is your intention to produce a raise. An intention is not at all like a want. In fact, intending to get something and wanting something are at opposite ends of the scale when it comes to producing results.

A want is something that you don't have now, something that you feel incomplete or unfulfilled about not having. It comes from a negative place because it's based upon a lack instead of a goal. Nine times out of ten, you don't have a want; it has you. It keeps you stuck and shut down. If you think getting what you want will satisfy you, you're in that nine-out-of-ten group.

An intention, on the other hand, is wholly unmotivated. It doesn't come from any currently existing external situation or any hidden internal agenda. It comes out of nothing and produces results just because you say so. That may not sound rational to you right now, but read the next few pages carefully. Then you'll see why rationality and reasonableness may have nothing to do with it.

Intention happens at a level outside of your ordinary awareness. It is used to determine the course and direct the outcome of events in your life and to bring events and other things into reality.

When you are in touch with that particular level of awareness, each new event becomes an opportunity for new experiences instead of the same old problems and surprises or other people overlooking you that same old way.

When you realize that you use your power of intention to actually choose the events that you experience, you can then choose between being satisfied and nurtured by what happens to you or being victimized, angered or depressed by it.

Either way, you always get what you intended. Always. And in all ways.

Here is how to discover the way intention works. And how to use it specifically and concretely in a way that will be easy on yourself and all the people around you. Including your boss.

Before you begin the process of putting in for a raise, make up a game. Give the game a name. Call it "Getting A Raise." Then bring all of your resources and talents into the game in a way that ensures winning.

It's easier done that said.

Just follow these steps.

Set up the game. The game is "Getting A Raise."
Whose game is it? Yours.
That's right. Never forget that it is your game. And that you get to say who wins and who loses. And how.

Set up the rules. The game will last 60 days if you say so. Is 60 days OK with you? If not, how many days is OK? Good.

The game ends when you have a raise. To win, the raise must be an increase up to at least the next appropriate level or 10 to 15 percent higher than your present salary. All right? To be a big winner, the raise must be _____. Fill in your own Go-For-It figure. For the entire period of the game, you agree to play full tilt. No holding back. No saving some for next time. Those are the rules.

Now, whose rules are they? Are you sure? From now on, please make it a point to always remember that the rules are your rules.

Check out the rules. Are you being too reasonable? Did you make the game too easy and boring? Or did you make it too hard and demanding? For some people, going for even a 10 percent raise could cause a major confrontation. For others, it's hardly worth the effort. Quite a few of the people I spoke with played flat-out and doubled their salaries in less than a year. (Later on, I'll tell you how they accomplished it.) Quite a few others were overjoyed with an additional ten dollars a week.

The point is not to limit yourself. And, on the other hand, not to make yourself crazy.

Just for the record, a difficult game with higher stakes is no better than an easy game played for penny ante. It's also no worse. As long as you're making up the game, make the game challenging and fun.

Be sure you can live with your rules and play by them without trying to change the set-up somewhere in the middle or near the end of the game. If you are anywhere in between an easy win and an impossible dream, you're probably in the right place.

Check out yourself. Are you willing to take full responsibility for your game and its creation? Are you really willing to follow the rules, your rules? Are you really willing to play flat-out for 60 days? Are you really willing to bring 100 percent of you into the game? That means bringing in all your fears about rejection, all your hidden beliefs about money, all your past screw-ups, all your anger about bosses and other authority figures, all your hopes, all your unpaid bills and all your other stuff. All of it has to be brought into the game. It's all part of you, therefore it's all part of your game, and you have to be aware of it all. Be certain you have identified as much of that as you can, so you know what you are including.

Declare yourself. Tell everyone you know (except your co-workers and supervisor if that's not appropriate) that you are going to get a raise by the date you chose. And tell them all exactly how much of a raise it will be. Go into detail and talk about what you will buy with some of the extra money and where you might go to celebrate.

Once you declare your intention by creating the game and once you make it a reality by committing yourself to it and sharing it with others, there is no turning back.

So watch out.

You are setting in motion the machinery that will enable you to materialize whatever it takes to win your game.

In the beginning, there is always the word. In the beginning of getting your raise, there is your word. You give your word about what you are going to do. Then you keep your word. By going out and doing what you said you would do. After that, you get to take satisfaction in the results.

When you create your own game, you can arrange everything so that the raise you get is the raise you want. And certainly not the raise a table of industry averages or a company acountant says is the right raise for you.

The national media have reported a number of different average raise figures for 1982. Most were between 5 and 7 percent. Most also say that employers will only give raises of about 5 percent per year in the future.

But remember; you're not a statistic. Statistics don't support you. Still, they are disappointing. So you may want general guidelines.

If you really want a target figure or benchmark raise to use in your game, here's what to do.

Make a good guess or actually find out what the employees one step higher than you on your company's ladder are earning. Then, simply shoot for that figure. Armed with this book, you'll find getting a raise like that is easier than you think.

However, if you investigate what the people on the next step are making and it's not enough for you, stick with this book and choose your own figure. You'll learn how to get it. Or, if you're in a small company and there's no one above you, pick a figure that is at least 15 percent higher than your present salary. If that's not enough, aim for more.

Once again: It's your game. Design and play it to get the raise you want, not the raise someone else says you ought to have.

Using your power of intention is the one and only way you have to be in complete charge of the process and take absolute responsibility for getting a raise. You can do this without ever being tossed and buffeted by fate, conditions, circumstances and other people.

Intention is the way to take over and own the whole experience, the way to make it your own game, the way to bypass the traps of asking, deserving, hoping or waiting for a raise while someone else controls the outcome, when you're playing someone else's game.

And what you need to remember is that if you don't choose to become the cause of your experience and take full responsibility for creating every bit of it every moment of every moment, you will be stuck with the alternative. And that is to be at the effect or the result of whatever happens to you next. With reaction as your only recourse instead of creation as your only choice.

You'll know when you are not in control because it will look as though someone else is doing something to you. And you will feel done in and swept under by the events of your life.

Get in touch with your intention right now. Then use it and this chapter as a foundation. It is the only foundation strong enough to fully support you in getting a raise in 60 days.

HOW TO GET MORE MONEY

- Make getting your raise something you really want to do. That way it's never hard.

- Align your whole self with your intention. That's the way to be successful.

- Become aware of all the ways that intention is different from want.

- Set up your Get A Raise Game. Then stick to the rules.

4

All About Money

The simple shocking truth about money is this: You don't have enough of it because you are caught up in a set of internalized beliefs that will never allow you to have enough of it. Not now and not ever. Certainly not as long as your beliefs remain frozen in place.

The trap that keeps you stuck without enough money is the way you have unconsciously accepted certain mass beliefs including what "everyone thinks" and what "everyone knows" about money. The problem is that you are not thinking the issues through on your own.

There is nothing wrong with buying into a mass belief. But in this case, it keeps you stuck, keeps you dissatisfied about money and keeps you trying to get it in ways that usually don't produce the desired result.

To clearly see what all that means, turn to page 40. Or write "The problem with money is:" on a blank piece of paper.

Then write down everything you believe to be a problem for you about money. Be sure to include any religious, economic, or philosophical positions or ideas about money that flash across your mind. List whatever comes up, including mottos and sayings such as "the root of all evil" and "the rich get richer." Also include anything you remember your mother or your father telling you about money while you were growing up, especially if any of it sounded as if it were a problem. Finally, include whatever you would say to your best friend right now regarding where you are in relation to money. And add whatever you imagine your best friend would say to you in reply.

Tell the truth. And take the time to do this exercise as completely as you can before reading any further.

The problem with money is:

_____

_____

_____

_____

_____

_____

_____

_____

_____

_____

_____

_____

_____

_____

All by itself, this simple list will remove one of the major obstacles that stands between you and a bigger paycheck.

As you look over the list of things you consider to be problems associated with money, you will notice one or more of the following recurring themes beginning to emerge.

Theme One: Money is a reward or an exchange or a kind of feedback resulting from something you have to do to acquire it.

Theme Two: Money is scarce and you have to compete for your share of some fixed or currently available supply of it.

Theme Three: Money is, at best, a necessary evil and it has the inherent power to corrupt moral values.

Buying into Theme One is unproductive. It locks you into a chain of reactions to external conditions and circumstances that seldom have anything to do with money.

When you think money is a reward or an exchange or a feedback measurement resulting from something you do for the purpose of receiving money, it always looks as though you have to do whatever you do more or better or differently to get more money.

That means that if you sell forty-five green bricks a week and you work eight hours a day and you earn ninety dollars a week, it looks as though you have to sell more green bricks or work more hours or develop a better sales presentation or do your job differently if you want to get a raise and earn more money.

That's not so.

The biggest, most satisfying raises are never created by looking for more or better feedback or a greater reward for your efforts. They are always the result of breaking free of traditional patterns of action and reaction.

For instance: You could open up a new territory. Or move up to the position of national sales manager for your company. Or start your own company. All of which might offer a greater return than continuing to do the same job just as you have always done it, but with a new, more, better or different twist.

Looking at money from a closed-loop feedback-and-reward system means that you can never take responsibility for directly creating it yourself. You can't because you are always waiting around for someone else to notice what you're doing and then to give you something for it.

Everything in your experience becomes second-hand that way. And out of your control.

Would you be willing to give up the idea that money is a reward or feedback device if it meant you could have more money from now on?

You certainly would.

Buying into Theme Two or the belief that money is scarce and you have to compete for it is just as unproductive.

Operating out of any premise that limits you is a lot like attempting to win the hundred-yard dash with a two-hundred-pound weight shackled to your ankle.

The idea that money is scarce just isn't true. Lots of people have lots of money. Just take a look around.

Banks are full of money. Millionaires' pockets are full of money. Your company has enough money to pay everybody every week and show a profit. And people who don't have as much money as you do think that *you* have lots of money. So it is not really scarce at all.

Money only seems to be scarce to you because of the way you have been looking at it.

Chances are, you believe there is only one pie and that everyone is only entitled to his or her fair slice of it. That's not how it works at all.

There are actually an unlimited number of pies out there. And an even more unlimited number of ways to bake as many more of them as you would like.

Once you realize that, you can have a pie that's all yours without taking anything away from anyone else. You can begin to enjoy a full belly, a full wallet and a full life.

One way to prove that is to notice how new ideas always attract a new supply of money without taking it away from the good old traditional places. The telephone, personal computers, video games and insolvable cube puzzles are all good examples. Once invented and produced, they attract enormous amounts of money. Good new ideas always do.

Soon, you'll see how to generate your own new ideas out of what you learn about what your company needs and wants. And how you can profit personally from them.

For now, would you be willing to give up the idea that there isn't enough money to go around if it meant that you could have all the money you want?

Good.

Buying into Theme Three or a notion that money leads to negativity or corruption is even more unproductive than the other two themes because it cripples your inherent power to choose how you want your own life to be.

If there is anything on your list of problems about money that even hints at the possibility of money being the root of all evil or a source of unjustness, loneliness or alienation, do this. And do it right now.

Take whatever money you have in your wallet and set it on an empty table in front of you. Take off your watch. Put it on the table next to the money. Time yourself as you stare at your money for the next two minutes.

What did you see?

Was it a root? Was it unjust? Was it evil?

Probably not.

Probably it was just a pile of green paper or metallic coins.

That's all it ever is.

And whether it is used for good purposes, like charity, a night on the town or a Club Med trip to Guadeloupe, or for bad purposes, like charity, a night on the town or a Club Med trip to Guadeloupe, depends on you and your point of view.

Money is never the source of anything. It is always the means to an end. And never the end in itself, or never should be.

If any of this gives you a tense feeling or if you are skipping over this part too fast, go back and take another look at your money. Then begin to take a good look at who is really the source of everything you call good or everything you call evil in your life.

Guess who?

Too bad.

It always gets back to that. And the way you can always tell who is responsible for all the events in your life is to notice who is the only person always there whenever anything happens to you.

And that includes everything. Good or bad. Inspiring or disappointing. Virtuous or corrupt.

So would you be willing to give up the idea that money is evil or immoral if it meant that you could always have a really abundant supply of it?

Fantastic.

Now you are ready to handle money once and for all.

Chances are, the things about money that trouble you include unpaid bills, a near-limit VISA account, various debts and current shortages. Or, perhaps even tragic problems such as not enough money for food or clothing or rent or heat.

Do you remember who is responsible for creating those problems, even though it may not have seemed that way at the time?

There are probably other types of money problems you would *like* to have, such as not knowing what to do with it all. Payments due on the yacht and the Rolls. Moving up to a higher tax bracket. Having to open four more bank accounts because you have exceeded the limits again. Needing to hire an armored car to carry it all around.

Do you know who would be responsible for creating all those problems?

Once you clear away the confusion of old, unconsciously held beliefs, it becomes obvious that you are the source of all your financial problems. Even whatever barriers you have that prevent you from making the most of that.

From now on, you will decide which set of problems you choose to have.

The next step involves focusing your intention on the flow of money in your life.

If you are at all fuzzy about what intention is and how it works, go back to Chapter 3. Be sure you are clear about the difference between wanting something and intending to have it.

Remember that an intention works because you say so. And because your word is the highest authority there is, whenever you stick to it.

All the exercises in this chapter are necessary. Each is a link to freeing you from some of the stuff that has been coming between you and an abundance of money.

If you became aware of fatigue, boredom, anxiety or any other persistent emotion while you were filling in your lists, that was part of the process. It was also completely normal and to be expected.

Money is one of the two most highly charged subjects around. It always was and always will be. It is also one of the two most misunderstood subjects because it carries an incredibly wide variety of conflicting beliefs, attitudes, considerations, judgments and points of view. Just mention money and these conflicts will leap to the surface.

In case you were wondering, the other subject *is* sex. But that's another book.

The exercises you did were designed to show you where you are wired-in to self-limiting beliefs, attitudes, considerations, judgments and points of view. And that's all.

Even if you still like, enjoy, relish and choose to hold on to each of your previous positions about money, you can now get a raise anyway. And enjoy all the extras it produces.

It is necessary to first become aware of where the internal traps are. For you. Then avoid falling into those traps for the 60 days of your Get A Raise Game.

My own experience with money is that it is just like any other natural resource. Abundant and seemingly cyclical.

For me, money has the potential of being as widely available as green grass and green leaves, which, in New England where I live, are everywhere you look for about six months of the year. It is also there the other six months, but like the grass and leaves, it is below the surface, unseen and regenerating.

You are the only limiting factor in how many leaves and lawns you can observe at one time and whether you see the whole green effect or one blade of grass or one single leaf at a time. You are also the only limiting factor in how much wealth you choose to have.

The important thing to remember is what each of the three recurring themes about money will cost you whenever you accept them blindly.

They cost you money.

And what you don't want them to cost you right now is the raise you are going to get in 60 days.

HOW TO GET MORE MONEY

- Examine your preconceptions and fears about money.
- Decide how much money you really want. Then choose how much money you really intend to have.
- Become aware of the internal traps that your own attitudes toward money produce.

5

What Your Company
Needs and Wants

By now, if you understand that getting a raise is 100 percent
your responsibility and 100 percent within your control,
you're on the right track.

You are also on the right track if you're beginning to see
that what you are doing at work right now is probably why
you haven't been getting abundant raises.

At best, what you do at work is whatever you think your
job is. And that may have nothing at all to do with what you
were actually hired to do in the first place.

"One of the things I'm aware of around here," says the
president of a medium-sized manufacturing company, "is that
most of my employees are doing what they feel they ought
to do to please their supervisors. They're working out of their
heads instead of finding out what really needs to get done
for the place to run more smoothly and profitably.

"I'm ready to give raises and bonuses to anyone who's willing to come up with a way to turn all that around."

All it may take for you to get a raise in 60 days, or a whole lot less time than that, is this.

Use this page, or take out a blank piece of paper. At the top, write a heading that says, "What I do at work."

Then write down everything you do that you think your job includes. Include everything that you actually do at work. Don't forget those things that may not be part of the official description of your job as it might appear in the company's employee manual. Don't include anything that you'd like to do or think that you ought to do. List only the actual elements of your daily job.

And don't leave anything out.

If what you do includes getting coffee for your boss or feeding the company goldfish, list that. Avoid evaluating what's important and what isn't.

When you are done, tell your supervisor that you want to see him or her about a personal matter.

What I do at work:

_____

_____

_____

_____

_____

_____

_____

_____

_____

_____

Start your discussion by acknowledging that you have been reviewing the various elements of your job so that you can improve your efficiency. Tell your supervisor how you have approached your work until now and mention all the elements on your list.

By this time, your supervisor will probably be telling you that some of the elements of your job should not be handled by you, that you should be doing some things that you are not, that some of the systems you use should be replaced. More than likely, your supervisor will be surprised that you're really doing as much as you are. If he or she doesn't say anything, you should ask for clarification about any areas of misunderstanding.

Raises and other miracles come from that process with no effort at all. So do it within the next two days, before you forget.

All you are doing is simply finding out what your employer wants and needs from you. Then do whatever that is. Instead of whatever else you have been doing.

Finding out what's needed and wanted is the only sure way to discover how to win. On your job. And in your life.

Lots of things are wanted and needed at work. They range from someone being available for an extra fifteen or twenty minutes a day to test a new work procedure to someone being able to suggest a way to avoid a production bottleneck, save money, increase efficiency and generate more profit from whatever job you do. The fact that it is your job makes you the ideal person to evaluate it.

What you have to do is just dig in and uncover all the conceivable possibilities. Do it as if it were homework. Because it will be the homework that produces your raise, it will turn out to be the most rewarding homework you've ever done.

It's not even hard to do. Wherever you work, you can always find dozens and dozens of things that are wanted and needed. Things that, as soon as you provide them for your employer, will earn you instant acknowledgment and even faster money.

How do you go about finding out what they are so you can do them?

Lots of ways. And through lots of different sources.

The best source is you.

Start looking at your job and your area of work as if you were your boss. Check around and notice what's wrong. Then ask yourself, if this was your company how would you fix whatever you found wrong.

Then share some of your conclusions with your supervisor.

You don't have to give everything away all at once. And if you do, and if your supervisor takes your ideas and claims them, don't complain about it or set out to get even or make him or her wrong. Instead, go back to the beginning and see what else needs fixing and find a way to fix it. Then share that with your supervisor again.

It doesn't matter who gets the credit. That's an essential notion to remember. Your game isn't about getting credit. Your game is getting a raise. And once you become known as the best damn source of workable solutions in the place, your value goes up fast. And so does your salary.

Another source is printed material.

You would be surprised how much you can find out about what your company needs and wants from the marketplace, the economy, the government and the workforce and staff (including guess who) just by reading. News magazines, trade journals, memos, annual reports and the company newsletter can tell you more than you think. Especially about how products are selling, what the profit picture is shaping up to be, and who's coming and going.

Occasionally the problem with using printed material as a source is that you learn what the media or the company wants you to learn instead of the truth. But even so, an item in the company newsletter that good old Sam Gronich is retiring can start you looking at how you might be able to fill his shoes and his pay envelope. And you can begin your end run for Sam's job without another moment's delay.

Still another source for finding out what's going on, what your company needs and wants, and what you can do about it, is other people.

The most common and widely available network of information is the company grapevine.

There is no doubt that fears, anxieties, hopes, stories and outright fantasies cling to the grapevine in large ripe clusters. But the company supervisors, managers and executives I spoke with all agree that between 75 and 80 percent of all the information making the rounds on the grapevine at any one time has some well-grounded support or a literal basis in fact.

The office manager of an accounting firm says "It's mouth-to-mouth communication. Fast, direct, totally anonymous. And the wildest rumors can be traced to a leak about something that's really in the wind. So it's insidious and uncontrollable. And so accurate that I use it myself."

No matter where you work, you will want to work the grapevine. If you are not already on one stem of it or another, take all necessary steps to connect with it. Not being on the grapevine is a sure sign that you're either dead, totally invisible or an endangered species.

One executive at a large office machine corporation uses the grapevine to his own advantage. "I can find out the latest stories about everyone in my department. I always know who's doing what, where the dissention, pregnancies and love affairs are and who's out looking around. I invariably use that kind of information before I make my decisions about raises or promotions."

Use that wisely. Sometimes you can plant constructive stories abut yourself and harvest the benefits later on.

The company grapevine is a useful communication tool. It has as many advantages as the telephone, so use it wisely and well.

Just don't use it to compete with other people. In fact, forget the idea that you are competing with your fellow workers for a raise.

You are not.

Getting a raise is not about competing. Competing is about competing. And getting a raise is about getting a raise.

This issue will keep coming up. So start to look at it now.

Consider it this way:

There is no scarcity of anything you want. That's true whether what you want is money or anything else. What makes it seem scarce is that you have been shortcircuiting yourself and your process of creating it on an intentional level by thinking that you have to compete for it when you really don't have to compete at all.

If all you do is what your company needs and wants for the next 60 days, you will get your raise.

What's more, you may inspire the people you work with to get raises too. Especially if you don't go about getting yours in a way that threatens them or that looks competitive to them.

When I was a department head at an advertising agency, there were two other department heads who formed the middle management level with me. Every time I got a raise, and I was a very aggressive raise seeker, they got the same raise. When I got to be a vice-president, they got to be vice-presidents. Everybody won each time I won. And I was never out to win at anyone else's expense.

The funny thing was they never wanted raises. They had the idea that raises meant you had to work longer or harder to keep on deserving them. So they were never as happy about it as I was. In fact, when they got raises by being promoted, they were angry with me. They didn't want the added responsibilities the promotions represented to them.

Barring competitiveness and inappropriate behavior, the grapevine is an excellent tool for getting a raise.

An expert at office politics at a television production company has thoroughly analyzed how it works. "Each reliable branch," she says, "includes three closely entwined tendrils: Secretaries, outsiders, and people on your own level. Data from each tendril will intersect somehow. And when it does, you know you've bypassed the new baby stories and the rumors about who's banging who in the supply room closet.

"When the intersection hits, you're always on to something big."

"Secretaries always know everything," says an executive secretary from corporate headquarters of a nationally known company that produces cameras and film. "Even when they won't tell, their body language or facial expressions can alert you to something being up.

"Cultivating a secretarial source is really easy. All you have to do is treat the one you want with professional respect and warmth. Oddly enough it's usually the women executives who make the worst enemies of secretarial grapeviners."

A shop foreman looks for his grapevine information outside his own company. He says, "Whenever I go to a trade meeting, the biggest trade of all is telling each other what we've heard about each other's plants. I get enough stories about who's drinking too much and which veeps are running around to program a soap opera for at least two weeks.

"And sometimes I find out about major shifts in my company's policies or products months before we'd get the word inside."

People who work at your level are the most useful and also the most difficult grapevine sources to cultivate. As the television production company political expert says, "It's all a big trade when you exchange information with your peers.

"They're after the same things you are, money and advancement, so you can usually count on them to leave something important out when they swap stories with you. That means you have to do the same. So it gets a little tough trying to remember who told what pieces to whom and what you're hanging on to yourself."

But apart from who you can tell what to, there has to be someone in the company you can rely on. Sometimes this person is an associate or corporate officer. Sometimes it's someone below you on the corporate ladder. Whoever it is, you need a company friend to support your intention to keep advancing at the company.

A company friend is today's equivalent of someone who takes on and holds down the roles of your teacher, your guide, your pal and your mentor.

Like a teacher, your company friend gives you all the facts and data about your job. Often the relationship starts when you are new to your job. From your company friend, you can learn little things, such as where the bathrooms are, and useful things, such as how actual management policy sometimes contradicts the employee manual data. That person can even teach you survival things, like avoiding meeting with the boss Friday afternoons after 2:30 or Monday mornings before 11:00.

Like a guide, your company friend shows you the ins and outs of everything that everyone else knows. Everyone else but you. This can include information about reliable grapevine terminals, how the company's power structure works, who's going up or coming down and where many of the dead ends and jackpots are hidden along the trails of the company maze.

Your company friend will align with you on what's good for both of you, act as a reciprocal sounding board for ideas and offer a warm receptive port in uncharted seas.

Like a mentor, your company friend can help make things happen for you.

Chances are, no one company friend will be able to handle all those roles at once.

You may want to cultivate two or three or four of them. It would even be possible for the person who takes on this role to work at a different company altogether. He or she may have the same job you have at another place and be able to align with you in a program of mutual aid and support. Or that person may even have had your job previously.

Are you wondering how to recruit your company friend or network of company friends?

Do it the same way you would enroll anyone into any relationship with you.

Be fully available and actively want the unique quality of support that company friendships can give you. That means don't hold back or send out mixed signals about your willingness to participate in the relationship. And don't shut down or go away whenever a potential company friend comes over to you.

Be sure that you genuinely like and trust the person or people you choose. Never try to fake it.

Whether your company friend is the same gender you are or not, avoid sex and any other highly charged emotional activity. If that's impossible, change the nature of the friendship from company to personal. Don't try to do both unless you are interested in finding out how it feels to be a two-way loser.

A classic case in point is now called "L'Affaire Bendix" and is beginning to be studied in corporate power and politics courses and MBA programs from coast to coast.

It began when William Agee, chairman of Bendix, took on the role of mentor to a young, female business school graduate. They worked together, went on business trips together and were seen together at large media events. Both were in the process of divorce or separation.

In an amazingly short time, the woman was promoted to vice-president. Despite denials, rumors surfaced that the two were having an affair and that the woman, Mary Cunningham, owed her advancement to Agee's attentions. Eventually, Cunningham resigned.

Agee and Bendix attempted the takeover of another company. The other company turned around and tried to take over Bendix. In the middle of all this, there were charges that

Cunningham was involved. Stockholders were outraged that someone outside the company was involved in merger discussions. Another company came to Agee's aid and saved Bendix, but his position was made redundant and he resigned.

If there is a silver lining to this story it is that Agee and Cunningham were married. While the two seem to be very happily married, the cost to their reputations was high.

The moral is obvious. Find out in advance what the price of your friendship is going to be. If taking the relationship to a personal level will mean a high cost to you, be sure you can afford it.

It could be simple sharing or thanks. Or a favor later on in your career. Or you taking up the banner of your friend's corporate point of view and carrying it into the future as if it were your own. This last price is frequently asked by an older person who has strong positions about how things ought to be.

Trust your intuitions about the cost of a company friendship. If you're unsure about anything, discuss it with your mentor.

Use whatever information network you have to find out whether or not your potential company friend is already someone else's company friend. If so, you need another confidant.

You can have more than one company friend, if you can handle it.

If you are lucky, one person may be able to fill most of the roles. If not, cultivate someone older and higher on the ladder to be your mentor, someone on your level to be your friend and a well-connected secretary or someone who's about to retire to be your teacher and guide.

Whichever type or combination of types of company friend you have, you have to give as much as you receive. As in all relationships, if it's very one-sided, the relationship will soon end.

Each type of company friend is relatively easy to find except the mentor. That person will require a strong reason to be enrolled. And he or she will enter into the relationship slowly and gingerly.

Since you have a lot to gain from a mentor, the relationship is well worth whatever effort it takes to create it. Here are some things you can do to help it along.

Find out all about the person you have chosen: Personal likes and dislikes. Political preferences. Major positions, points of view, biases. Lifestyle traits. Company contributions and successes. Family and educational ties. Community interests. Hobbies and sports. All of it.

The grapevine and his or her secretary are the best sources. But use both with care and delicacy.

Then begin to present the parts of yourself that genuinely fit the preferences of your prospective mentor. If you and your target for company friendship both love to fish, let it be known that you have invented a new kind of superfly that pulls them up when nothing else will or that you have access to a secret trout stream or something else that sounds just as irresistible.

Another way is to locate an obscure trade journal article that supports one of that person's favorite positions about something at work. Clip or copy it and drop it off at your potential mentor's office yourself. Tell how you heard about his or her interest in the subject, how you share that interest, how you came across this article in your reading and how you immediately thought of that person. Then leave right away. Let the connection form itself.

Still another way is to seek out that person for career counseling or advice. Be sure to do it in a way that does not look as if you are trying to bypass your immediate supervisor. It may be necessary for you to make your initial approach outside of the office at a racquetball club, a political rally or some other favorite spot where your friend likes to go. If your target mentor is not of the same sex, be sure to define the parameters of the relationship. Remember the Bendix case. Be sure you're willing to accept the consequences of your actions. And be sure to keep the relationship on a professional level if that's your true aim.

Whichever approach you use, once your potential company friend sees that you are made of the same stuff that he or she is, you will be on your way. Just expect it to take time and continuous validation before the friendship becomes rock solid.

Once formed, company friendships, especially mentor relationships, must be handled with the same care and nurturing you would devote to any other relationship.

And be sure to always remember the purpose of a company friendship.

The purpose is not to have it be part of your Get A Raise in 60 Days game plan. In fact, it will probably take considerably longer to cultivate a company friend than it takes to get a raise.

The purpose of a company friendship is to provide you with background data and support in finding out specifically what your company needs and wants. Which in the long run can be a bigger kettle of fish than just this one raise.

You see, once you are permanently connected to knowing what's needed and wanted, you can continuously focus and refocus your resources and your experience to provide it. You can even put yourself in charge of seeing that it gets handled on every level.

And once you do that, you won't need this book anymore. What you'll need will be a better accountant.

HOW TO GET MORE MONEY

- Discover what your company wants and needs. Then provide it.
- Make getting a raise your responsibility and realize that it's within your control.

abits, so he frequently anticipates errands and
e's even available for playing racquetball with
regular partners can't keep a date.
erforms his job at a much higher level than
lways the one I think of first for extra money
review time.
is, both Dave and Jimmy are my partner's
at happens is that Dave is always getting
immy."
u're one of the boss's kids, you'll want to work
measurable level you can. Someone like Dave
es wherever he worked. Someone like Jimmy
ld not.
ervisors I spoke with base your raises, at least
xtras involving your personality and your
get along with other people who work with
sn't mean excessive socializing, by the way.
ing and social activity work against you and
as much as hiding out and being the company

is to achieve that special and somewhat delicate
ncludes being genuinely interested in other
er work opportunities around you while being
oing your own job completely and being open
most of the time.
what kind of job you have, that takes the form
ing "Good morning" and "Good night" to
see on the way in and out, and occasionally
e else's coffee or bringing in a few doughnuts
ins to share. And generally being an open and
.
or on an assembly line confided that "This one
is doing little extra things, not to get people
because he likes people. You can always tell
He even loaned me money a couple of times
ittle short. Naturally I paid him back.

- Discuss what you do in your job with your boss. Clarify and correct any misunderstandings.
- Look to yourself, company publications and other workers to find ways to make yourself and your job more efficient.
- Cultivate the corporate grapevine.
- Look for and develop a company friend or friends.

and person
coffee calls
me when

"Dave
Jimmy. He
whenever i

"Prob
kids. So v
raises...fo

Unless
on the high
would get r
probably w

Most s
in part, on
willingness
you. That d
Too much t
cost you rai
phantom.

The tric
balance that
people and o
professional,
and availabl

No matt
of always sa
everyone yo
buying some
or English mu
friendly pers

A superv
fellow always
to like him bu
the difference
when I was a

Gettir

t

"The thing I notice m
they do their work
whatever their job sp
officer of a large leg

"For instance, t
the same job. It's a
includes everything
for coffee to getting

"Jimmy brings a
He does whatever y
sometimes. He hides
without saying muc
to anyone when he

"Dave is just th
checks in with eve
volunteers extra hel

"Just as naturally, whenever it's time to put in my recommendations for raises, his name is always at the top of my list.

"You could say I want to make extra certain that we keep him around because his attitude's so great. He definitely makes a big difference in my section of the plant."

Want to evaluate your job right now and see how it's working for you?

Complete the evaluation form on page 70.

There are no right or wrong answers.

The idea is just to tell the truth and notice how you feel. You will have a clear indication right away about your attitude toward your job. By examining this chart, you can easily see whether your attitude toward your job is conducive to getting a raise.

It's almost painfully obvious. If you catch a lot of colds, feel angry or sad most of the time and see a rat-like figure when you think of your boss, don't expect a raise this year or next. If you feel energetic every morning, exercise after work and rate your aliveness at 10, count on extra money soon.

Your attitude has a lot to do with where you are in relation to handling all your stuff. If you took care of it by doing the exercises in Chapter 2, you don't need to worry about it now.

Your attitude about work is important because it's what your boss sees every time he or she looks at you. And your attitude tells your boss if you are happy with your job. Or if you're not. And that seems to be important to your boss.

I want you to know that it doesn't really matter whether you are happy with your job right now or not.

There is a way to get happy with your job and to get the rewards and raises that go with what looks like on-the-job happiness, even if you think you hate it.

The first thing to do is to acknowledge that your job doesn't look as good to you as it did the day you first got it. You should also acknowledge that other jobs, particularly the one you are going to get next or someday or whenever, look a lot better than the one you have now.

If that is true for you, now is the time to look at it and to examine exactly what that means. And what it costs you.

What it means is that where you are right now isn't good enough to be an end in itself. And it certainly isn't good enough to be considered an ultimate experience.

So you are going around with a sense that something else that's better will come along and change your life and your working career for the better.

The problem is, that never happens.

After all, how many jobs have you had already? And how many times was it always the next job that would be the perfect job for you? The one that would make you happy to wake up every morning and happier yet to show up at the company door.

That pattern is deadly.

No kidding. It is literally killing you by making your life heavy, sad, slow moving and petty paced.

What it costs you is satisfaction, joy, enthusiasm and aliveness. All of those are the qualities for which most employers are anxious to pay you handsomely.

Do you want to dissolve that pattern forever?

Are you sure?

It's actually easy to do once you are actually willing to do it.

Here's how.

Stop living your life as if something better is going to come along and save you.

It won't.

Even if whatever you hope will happen actually does happen, it won't last.

When you are stuck wanting something else, you will always want something else. No matter how many something else's you get, none of them are enough. And none of them will ever be enough for you.

Instead, start to live your life as if it is exactly what you want. Beginning with your job.

Whenever you want exactly what you have, you can get a lot of satisfaction out of it. And it is the kind of satisfaction you never notice when you are waiting for the next thing to come along.

Go back and read those last four paragraphs again.

Maybe you can't think of enough reasons to want what you have now.

So forget all about reasons.

Just look at your shoes, your dog, your cassette player and whatever else you have in your life and begin to want all of it just the way it is.

Next, look at your job and all the equipment and the people and the procedures and begin to want all that just the way it is.

Get the idea that it is the perfect place for you to experience and share who you are. Also, accept the idea that it is the perfect place to expand your life and your income.

And as soon as you stop making it wrong and stop looking for a better or different or more perfect place to show up, your job will be perfect. Right now. Just the way it is.

Try it.

It's not hard to do. In fact, it gets to be easier and easier as you go along. And it also gets to be so satisfying you won't be able to believe it.

It's not magic. And it's not doubletalk. It's simply accepting things as they are, then creating them any way you choose.

The next step is to create a way to maintain an unbelievably high level of satisfaction for the full 60 days of your Get A Raise Game.

The only way to do that is for you to be willing to agree that accepting your job as it is will be the way it is going to be for you. Then you need to formalize your willingness to have it that way with a list of agreements that you can use to support yourself in keeping your word. Consciously and completely.

At first, agreements sound as if they are something like rules and regulations. They are not.

Rules and regulations always come from someone or somewhere other than yourself. Agreements are simply whatever you give your word to do or not to do. Rules and regulations are usually all about not doing something that someone else says you shouldn't do. Invariably, they are the cause of most of the wrongmaking and wrongdoing in the world. Agreements, on the other hand, are a statement about your intention to have things work.

Since you are serious about getting a raise in 60 days, take out a blank piece of paper and write "My agreements about work" at the top.

The following suggested agreements about work and principles of working will apply to you whether you are a hard-hat or a hard-headed executive. So copy each one down on your list.

1. I agree to make these agreements my own agreements and to keep them.

2. I agree to have the job I have and to take complete responsibility for choosing to have it just the way it is.

3. I agree to be responsible for producing results and creating satisfaction for myself and value for my employer.

4. I agree to organize my job so that I can produce results for my employer during normal working hours.

5. I agree to accept my employer's rules about absence and lateness and to make them my own agreements, and to communicate responsibly about any exceptions. If I notice a lot of exceptions coming up, I agree to accept the responsibility for my absences or latenesses to work or coming back from lunches and breaks and look into why I am making it that way.

6. I agree that my purpose at work is to work and I agree to participate in my work at a 100 percent level during working hours.

7. I agree to handle any complaints I have at work or about my work by speaking directly to someone who can do something about them. I agree not to accept complaints from anyone else unless I can do whatever it takes to correct the problem. Instead, I will direct all complaints that come my way to whomever can take care of them with direct action.

8. I agree to look at all problems and obstacles to experiencing satisfaction at work as new and exciting opportunities to overcome barriers that in the past would have prevented me from wanting my life exactly the way it is.

9. I agree to remain conscious about who is responsible for me keeping my agreements. When I break an agreement, I will acknowledge what I have done and take whatever steps are appropriate to correct the break or clean up the mess. And then I will re-commit myself to keeping my agreements. Without making myself wrong or feeling guilty.

Check now and see what else you would like to make agreements about that relate specifically to you or your job. There's room on your list for a couple more.

You might want to add agreements about keeping your work area clean or being ruthlessly honest about your expense account or whatever else may come up for you right now.

Check now to see whether you are putting down or skipping over this process of making agreements. Everyone on the planet has been breaking agreements covertly or openly for the last five thousand or so years. That just may have something to do with why things don't seem to work very well these days.

If you are willing to focus on these few small agreements about your job for the next 60 days, just as an experiment in workability, the results will amaze you. And that doesn't just mean the part about the raise you'll get. Try it and see for yourself.

Get back to your list and be sure it is complete.

Then keep it where it is handy and accessible. You will be using it again and again and again. It is one of your strongest weapons in launching your campaign for a quick raise.

Your agreements will totally reinforce your intention to have your job be an absolutely satisfactory experience.

And because there are so few consciously kept agreements anywhere in the world, your list will serve you doubly by being exactly one of the things your employer needs and wants.

Creating satisfaction 100 percent of the time by having your job be the one all-time-great job is a guaranteed way to move your performance level up to the stratosphere, to have your work really work for you and to keep winning company popularity contests.

If you can't do that because you're convinced that your job is not the greatest job in the world and you still want to get a raise, here's the answer: For the next 60 days, pretend it *is* the greatest job in the world. Act accordingly. You'll be surprised. At the end of 60 days, you may not be acting.

As you will soon find out, people who are satisfied with whatever they have right now attract large amounts of esteem and admiration from everybody they encounter. And they are not actually doing anything else any differently.

It is the easiest way of all to handle the "getting along" issue at work. And getting the raise that goes along with it.

HOW TO GET MORE MONEY

- Be friendly and open. Say "Good morning" and "Good night" to everyone you see.

- Accept your job as it is. Then make it the best job in the world.

- Make formal agreements with yourself about your conduct, attitudes and performance standards at work. Then keep your agreements.

- Remember that you spend at least eight out of twenty-four hours in a working day at your job. Make that experience satisfying and rewarding.

JOB EVALUATION FORM.

1. When I wake up in the morning I feel:
   ( ) Energetic   ( ) Tired   ( ) Depressed

2. Generally my health is:
   ( ) Very good   ( ) OK   ( ) Not so good

3. Every year I usually manage to catch:
   ( ) 0-1 cold   ( ) 2-4 colds   ( ) 5 or more colds

4. My most consistent emotion is:
   ( ) Happy   ( ) Angry   ( ) Sad

5. On a scale of 1 to 10, I rate my aliveness at
   ( ) 10   ( ) 5 to 9   ( ) 0 to 4

6. When I think of my boss, my first image is:
   _____

7. After lunch, when I go back to work I feel:
   _____

8. The part of my body where I feel the most tension at
   work is: _____

9. I usually get about _____ headaches a week.

10. What I like to do most after work is:
    ( ) Take a seminar or class   ( ) Meet new people
    ( ) Exercise   ( ) Watch tv   ( ) Have a drink or two
    ( ) _____ ( ) _____

7

The Company Way

Traditional companies have traditional ways of handling raises, which usually involve periodic evaluations or reviews.

If you work for a company that follows these traditional patterns, and about 90 percent of all companies do, it may appear that you will never get a raise in 60 days unless your annual review falls within that period.

It may also appear that you are stuck. Stuck with a periodic review. Stuck with a fixed-percentage annual raise. Stuck in a raise bind you believe to be so fixed that no book or system could ever break you out of it. Even this one.

The good news is that's not so.

The bad news is that if you have a civil service job, a heavily-regimented departmentalized job, a closed-shop, union-controlled job, or any job where guidelines for raises are as rigid as railroad ties, you'll need to take a quantum leap to get the raise you intend to have.

But don't worry. This chapter will show you how to do it.

Start by taking a really close look at the mechanics of one of the traditional company ways that raises are given.

Once a year, each full-time employee is called in for a management review of his or her performance on the job and a determination of whatever raise may be appropriate. New employees are usually reviewed after their first three to six months.

Some companies have periodic performance reviews in between raise reviews. These may occur monthly or at longer intervals. Usually these are strictly a one-on-one experience with your immediate supervisor.

The annual review is usually handled by your supervisor and at least one or two higher-up management people. In smaller companies, the president or owner is often directly involved. In medium or larger companies, you seldom have contact beyond an operations manager or financial vice-president.

At best, company reviews will give you a great chance to blow your own horn about your contributions to the workability of your job. They will also give you an opportunity to look at management's idea of what your job is all about as opposed to whatever you may think your job is all about. If there is still any wide difference of opinion on that subject, your review is the perfect place to clarify any confusion.

At best, company reviews will also give you valuable feedback and a framework in which to see yourself at work as others see you.

The key is to listen. By listening closely and nondefensively, you can learn a lot.

You'll be able to listen without being defensive or argumentative if you keep reminding yourself that your review is supposed to be a learning experience. Nothing more. And after you have blown your own horn a little, you won't learn anything new unless you shut up, take it all in and thank your reviewers for sharing information with you.

The most important thing they'll be sharing, by the way, is what may be standing between you and a higher standard of living. So be sure not to miss that part.

If you feel compelled or driven to give excuses and justifications or otherwise defend your position, you won't learn anything. You probably won't get a great raise either. Not now or ever.

At their worst, company reviews are empty rituals. Management already knows what you are going to get for a raise. Usually it's a flat 10 percent or whatever the inflationary equivalent is that year. They call you in to an office and they tell you that you'll be getting the same raise as everyone else. Which means there's not a lot of opportunity to improve your role at work or your bottom-line take-home.

That's when it feels as if all you get to do is sit there and nod your head.

Whether you get the best of company reviews or the worst or somewhere in between, and there's a whole lot of room in between, just accept it all exactly the way it is.

It won't do you any good to go into the review and scream and yell about how unfair the company is. And it won't do you any good to make the company wrong.

This book is not about butting your head against the company review and trying to make it better or different or more fair. It is not even about taking any kind of stand about it at all. This book is about getting a raise.

Your company review will go more smoothly if you are prepared. The preparation techniques in Chapter 11 can assist you in making the most of your review. A review will not make you instantly rich, but being prepared will help you get the most out of it. The preparation will also help you feel more independent. You won't feel as if you are at the mercy of the person doing the review. And, you'll be able to rationally discuss anything that may come up in the review.

There's something else that might make you feel better during your review: Annual reviews don't work and management knows it.

The people who make the guidelines rarely agree on how to evaluate results. Programs tend to be inconsistent and haphazard.

One problem involves all the ways your bosses' reactions to your personality or style can color their appraisal of your performance. Whenever human beings evaluate other human beings, purely objective criteria are impossible to achieve.

Another problem is that performance evaluation generally has nothing at all to do with your raise. It has to do mostly with someone else's opinion about your performance.

Finally, scales of evaluation like one-to-ten or A-to-F are far too abstract, too arbitrary and too limiting to be the standard by which a year of hard work is reviewed.

The consequences of raise-review systems occasionally show up in highly dramatic ways.

One data processing department supervisor reports, "The results of our annual raise review system were so bad that we discovered a consistent 90 percent turnover rate every two years and an incredibly high cost of training new personnel.

"To reverse that pattern, last year in midyear we called everybody in and gave the whole department an across-the-board 15 percent raise.

"We're now in the process of coming up with a new and more individualized system that lets the employees become more actively involved in making the ultimate decisions about their own raises.

"Each one is also invited to target their next review date on the calendar and to be responsible for setting the performance improvement goals that will be used to determine the next salary increase.

"Turnover has dropped to less than 10 percent in the last six months and we anticipate that it will drop even lower than that. In addition, a fairly large raise pool has resulted from the money it used to cost to train replacement personnel."

Most companies are not as open to evolving and growing. And many companies will probably go right on with their current raise-review system forever. Or at least until twenty years after you get your gold watch and take off for Florida.

So if you choose to stay put, not change jobs and get your raise in 60 days anyway, you will have to operate outside of your company's traditional review system, without making that traditional review system wrong or trying to change or liberalize it in any way. And without ever putting down your company's management people for having such a tacky, old-fashioned, unfair, arbitrary system to begin with.

That last part is important. Be sure you are taking it in clearly and completely if you want to have the raise you want by the time you want it.

Your company's policies have to be absolutely all right with you. Or else you don't belong there. If you don't like the way things are done, the most that can ever happen is that your income and advancement prospects will slow down until they vanish all together. Then you'll have to leave.

It is really important to understand that you can operate effectively outside the limits of your company's review system without ever confronting that system directly, rebelling against it or putting it down.

Hundreds of department heads returned a questionnaire I prepared as part of my research for this book. One of the questions read: What would definitely prevent an employee from getting a raise?

The answer that appeared over and over was the word "Insubordination."

What the almost sixty people who gave this response on my questionnaire meant was this: The company way is the way the company operates. If you don't like it, get out.

It's that simple.

You see, when you first went to work for your company, you agreed on an implicit level to fit in and to work the way they hired you to work.

When you work for someone else, you don't get to vote about your job. They have the only vote. And the best way to keep your job working for you is to agree with that vote and do your job the way they tell you to do it.

Naturally, suggestions about improving efficiency and generating a higher profit will be welcomed eagerly. But only when they come from within the context of the job you were hired to do.

That's hard to take.

And it's the truth.

If you want to do your job your way instead of your company's way, what you need to do is start your own company. That way, you get the vote about how your job should be set up, how everyone else's job should be set up and how the system for raises ought to be run.

If you ever do start your own company and you hire someone to do a job that you created and they want to do that job their way instead of your way, will you give them a raise? Will you even keep them around long enough to collect dust?

Of course not.

Accept and enjoy your job just the way your company has set it up and just the way it is, without adding anything to it or taking anything from it.

When you do that, your on-the-job satisfaction will hit an all-time high. The company's way and your own way will be in a true state of alignment.

If you hear a little voice in the back of your head and that voice is saying anything like "I can't do that, my boss's way stinks" or "My company's way is terrible," simply notice that is the voice of your thoughts speaking. Remember what you now know about thoughts and stuff like that, then get down to the business at hand. That business is: Not just accepting your job, but beginning to love it just the way the company has set it up. Just the way it is. With nothing added to it and nothing left out.

To formalize that and to commit yourself to being in alignment with your company for the 60 days of your Get

A Raise Game, take out your list of agreements. Add this one to the bottom of the list:

I agree to accept and support the company way.

If you've been paying close attention, and I'm sure you have, you'll notice something that looks like a major contradiction.

It takes this form.

How can you accept and fully support the company's way of raise reviews and, at the same time, operate outside of it to get your raise in 60 days?

Very easily.

It involves a process of stepping back far enough to see the box that you're trapped in, the outside edges of the box and the next space around the box. All at the same time.

What does that mean?

Well, for the next few moments, pretend that you are one of the little inky black words on this page. You are surrounded by other words in a formation with well-ordered white spaces and white lines in between and all around. It's a flat two-dimensional world and you are an integral part of it. It's also an orderly, rigid system of lines and spaces, black and white. And being just a word on this page, there's nothing you can do to change your fate.

If you complain and disrupt the page enough by moving out of alignment with the words on your line, some proofreader will come along and boot you out and insert another more cooperative word that will hold down your place in the line within the system of the printed page. And that word will like being where it is.

Now once again pretend you are the same word on this page. You are still not willing to be limited by the system you are in, but you realize you have nothing to gain by not fully accepting the system of the page just the way it is. You know it won't do you any good not to accept and acknowledge the workability of the page's structure and orderliness and neatness.

Instead you choose to accept that system and to enjoy it exactly the way it is. And, to take care of yourself, because the essence of you is bigger than all that, you step back far enough from the page to be able to see the edges of the page along with the space around the page.

From your new point of view, you can see two hands holding the edges of the page, and the other things the person with those hands can see, hear, smell, touch and feel, in the room that the person holding the page occupies.

By stepping back to the next level of awareness, you create a transformational shift that frees you from the confining structure you were in. The two-dimensional page that kept you boxed in has now become part of an infinitely wider and expanded three-dimensional context. In this new context, you can enjoy and support the system of the page and still move freely and have comparatively limitless choices.

Obviously, you can keep stepping back to include whatever space you find yourself stuck in. You can create that same transformational shift as often as you want. And each time you do so, you expand to include infinitely more choices and personal freedom.

When the room becomes too small and too limiting, you can accept and enjoy that and simply step back to include the house or apartment the room is in. Then you can move freely again.

When the house or apartment becomes too small and too limiting, you can simply step back to include the block. Then the neighborhood. Then the town. And so on and so on and so on.

Whenever you find yourself boxed in by a system or any external circumstances, the easiest way out is to step back and create that next wider level of context and to enjoy all the space and freedom that goes with it.

You can create that kind of shift whenever you are not resisting whatever is happening in the space you are occupying. Whenever you are not justifying and defending your position or making other people wrong and responsible for your being stuck.

You always have that choice. To stay stuck and locked into limiting circumstances, or to step back to the next space or next wider context where you can again move freely.

So how does all that work at your company?

Like this:

Notice that you and everybody else at your company is stuck in a space as limiting as the pattern of words on this page must appear to each individual word.

The company way involves one raise review a year. And that's that. Resisting, complaining, rebelling or openly confronting the system will only get you fired or written in on the no-raise list with indelible ink.

Begin to become aware that you can't move freely and can't win on that level. Then accept everything on that level just the way it is. Unlikely as it may sound, accept and enjoy the way it is. Support it completely. Your company's review system is about as locked in place and as solidly constructed as the World Trade Center, so you might as well just relax and support it.

However, you can also step back to include the edges of the system and all the space around it. Widen your context so you can begin to operate freely and choose what's going to be next for you. Like a raise in 60 days.

The way to do that is to do your job just the way your company hired you to do it. And do it at that 100 percent level you said you would in your agreements.

In addition to that, look at what you are doing from your company's point of view and step back to shift your context to the next level of performance or responsibility.

That means: Do your job at the next level of effectiveness.

If you are a six-dollar-an-hour employee and you are playing your Raise Game for a one-dollar-an-hour raise, start working like a seven-dollar-an-hour employee works at your company. And do a seven-dollar-an-hour job the company way.

If you are a $30,000-a-year executive and you want to get a $10,000 raise, start working like a $40,000-a-year executive works at your company. And do a $40,000-a-year job the company way.

You are still playing by company rules, without complaining, rebelling or giving up. Only now, you have created an expanded context to operate in: a context so big that it transcends traditional raise-review system criteria.

In other words, you have made yourself bigger than your company's annual review system.

A few words of warning.

Don't make an enemy of your supervisor in the process of stepping back. Never, never do that.

When you promote yourself to the next salary level and then work at that level to get the salary that goes with it, you often run the risk of upsetting your supervisor.

Here's how to avoid that.

Find out the two or three things your supervisor likes the least about his or her job. Then volunteer to take over those areas of work, one at a time.

If your supervisor hates filing, after you have handled your own job, the next level for you is to say "I've got everything done and I have some extra time. Can I take over some of the filing for you? I love doing detail work."

If your supervisor hates using the telephone, after you have completed your own job for the day, your next level is to say "I've finished and I have a little extra time today. Can I make a few follow-up calls for you? I've been working on a more effective telephone presentation and I'd sure like to practice it."

You get the idea. Whatever your supervisor hates doing most, make that part of the expanded portion of your job. But get his or her blessings first. Then become really good at it so you can keep on doing it.

But what if you think you don't like your supervisor or feel that he or she does not deserve any extra help from you? Notice that this is just one more attitude you have. File it with the rest of your stuff and begin to become aware that it's very likely your attitude toward your boss that's been causing your problems with him or her. You can completely transform your attitude. And if you do, in almost all cases, your boss's attitude toward you will change.

"I used to think my boss was a jerk who didn't deserve a decent day's work," says the current marketing head of a large company. "If I did a first-rate day's work, my boss would get all the credit. And he was too big a jerk to deserve that. So I goofed off a lot. And I noticed that my boss goofed off a lot. And my lazy secretary, she even goofed off more than I did.

"Well one day I got the idea that I'd like to see my job work, so I took on the job of getting things done in my department even though my boss, who never encouraged me and never smiled, might get all the credit.

"I saw that if I stepped back into a large game, I'd get the benefits. And it wouldn't matter who got the credit.

"So I started working really hard. When someone wasn't getting their job done, I'd get it done for them. I began to feel like a reverse gremlin. Someone who would sneak in at night and fix all the machinery intead of sabotaging it.

"Within six weeks, I never saw my department running so smoothly. And I never saw my boss or my secretary working so hard.

"He still never smiled much and never encouraged me. But he started taking me to lunch a lot. And when he got promoted for having such a great department, he made sure that I got his old job."

Whenever you work harder, the one who gets the most out of it is you.

Ideally, you will wind up with an official promotion too. Within 60 days. And you will get the raise that goes with it. Completely outside of the company review system. Because the one almost universal exception to annual reviews are promotions.

Just a word or two about promotions. They are not the same as raises. They are better. Not only do they include more money, they also include more opportunity for you to expand the limits of your present job and make more of an impact on your company's management.

Here is an even simpler example of what you can do, related by an executive from the fashion world:

"When I was a graphic artist at a clothing company in an old building in the warehouse district, I had a rather unusual office. It was half closet-space and half work-space. I was crowded into the work-space half while this big dark closet was mostly full of old junk.

"One day I noticed that everyone on the floor was stepping on old patterns and crushing and tearing them. I got the idea that I could save the company the cost of having to redo the patterns if I could hang them somewhere. So I came in the next Saturday, cleaned out all the old junk in the closet part of my office, painted it white and hung two long racks in it.

"I started picking up the stepped-on patterns every day after work and hanging them in my closet. It took only about twenty minutes extra to do it. But before long, the production people started bringing them into my office for me and hanging them neatly on the racks I had built.

"I devised a filing system for them and kept eveything organized and neat. I liked doing it because it gave the unused part of my office some purpose.

"After awhile, I had a lock put on the door to the closet at my own expense so I could keep order. Of course, I had the keys.

"It didn't take long for the company's creative vice-president to notice that I was doing a job that needed doing and that no one had ever done before.

"So I got an additional title of Creative Administrative Assistant. And I got a $750 raise on the spot.

"I know I set it up all myself. And I'm about to do it again. With opportunities like the ones I can dream up all around, I mean, why wait!"

The way to your next raise is wide open.

It's the company way. Only it is a newly expanded version of it that comes from a much wider context. And you can make it work for you. In 60 days.

HOW TO GET MORE MONEY

- Make your salary review an educational experience.
- Prepare for your review. Do homework. Be ready to discuss your contributions.
- Step back to an expanded level of awareness whenever you feel trapped in a box or limited by procedures. Keep stepping back to create a context in which you have more room to operate.
- Do your job at the next higher level of effectiveness and you'll soon receive the next level of salary.
- Accept and enjoy the company way. Don't make it wrong.

8

Getting Personal and Other Long Shots

From all those good old black-and-white movie comedies of the thirties to your choice of any of the current crop of highly explicit soaps, the adventure and lure of love and sex at work has been a favorite theme.

Marrying the boss, hooking up with the chairman's daughter or son, being available for nooners or cocktails and dinner and lovemaking after a hard day on the job, even quickies in the Xerox room, have all been romanticized as sure ways to fame, fortune and advancement.

Don't believe it.

Getting personal with your supervisor or anyone else where you work just does not work. It actually never did work. And today, it's even riskier than ever.

To begin with, any dating, sexual or romantic relationship is normally a highly intense and emotionally charged experience. Unless you and your lover are either superhuman or supershallow, the odds of maintaining any sense of objectivity in a working environment that includes other people is next to impossible.

There is simply no way to keep what you are up to a secret. No matter how hard you try for privacy, everyone else always knows what's going on. Just like you almost always know when any other two people at your company are involved.

One of the things everyone knows is that you will never treat your lover the same way you treat your lover's competitors. And vice versa. And the higher up one or the other of you is, the more threatening that becomes to everybody else.

While you're seeing hearts and flowers, everyone else will be seeing one of you either seeking an advantage or getting one.

So save sex for after hours.

It is one of the long shots that doesn't produce a raise in 60 days.

Another long shot that doesn't work is changing jobs.

No matter what you have heard or what you think, it's not the way to get a raise. It is the way to get another job.

Changing jobs may have the effect of producing a fatter bottom-line salary for you. But it's a lot more work than playing your Get A Raise Game for 60 days. And after you get another job, you still have to handle getting a raise after you get there. No matter what your new salary is, unless you deal with some of the issues involved in setting up a Raise Game, it will never be enough.

If you don't learn how to get frequent and satisfying raises wherever you are, you will have to keep changing your job every year. And that will eventually have a way of hurting your marketability.

Getting another job and holding your present boss up for a counter-offer is not the way this system is set up. For that reason, any raise you get for leaving your job lacks integrity.

My own experience has shown that if the only way you can get your boss to raise your salary is by leaving, it's time to leave. And time to find a boss who will reward you fairly for your contributions instead of bleeding your energy unfairly until you are ready to pack up your marbles or lose them.

I once got a 40 percent raise for turning down a better-paying job. I saw that I was at a dead end after three years at an ad agency where I was vice-president and creative director. So I went out and got a better job with a 40 percent salary increase as VP/Creative Director at a larger ad agency. I never did leave to start that other job.

My boss followed me all around the office and out to lunch every day for a week after I gave notice that I was leaving. He even followed me home one evening and stayed all night, talking me out of leaving and making such outrageous promises that I stayed.

The raise wasn't worth it. As comfortable as I was at that company, that job was truly a dead end. And promises are only as good as the person who promises them. So while I wasn't sorry I stayed, I wasn't glad either. And two years later I got out.

Sometimes you don't actually have to look for another job to get a counter-offer. And that's the only time that kind of raise is worth getting.

I remember a series of unexpected raises that I got at my first advertising job. Each one was a real surprise until I figured it out.

I began to realize that each time the head of the company saw me in the hall talking to a departing account executive, I'd get a thousand-dollar raise on the spot. I was only saying goodbye and sharing well wishes for the future. But it must have looked as if I was being pirated away.

It was a great game. I made sure I was seen talking with each and every departing account management person. And I actually doubled my starting salary in less than two years.

The fact that I was doing a great job writing copy didn't hurt of course. But the point is, I never did have to look for another job until it was chronologically time to move on.

Getting the benefits of a counter-offer without putting in the time and effort it takes to get another job (even when you use my *Get A Job in 60 Seconds* system) is one of the few long shots that works. But because it's tricky and calls for an unusually high sense of your own self-worth, I suggest you stick with the Raise Game techniques that are outlined step by step in Chapter 10.

Still another usually unworkable long shot is the dynamite idea. There is a widespread myth that if you have a great idea, you'll get rich quick.

You may. But not at your company.

As far as your company goes, dynamite ideas mean trouble and change. The larger your company is, the more certain that is.

Conservative ideas that raise sales 10 or 15 percent. Innovative ideas that save three production steps out of the twenty that are normally required to turn out a part. Useful ideas that eliminate unnecessary paperwork. All those will get you your raise.

But dynamite ideas that set your industry on its ear probably won't get you anything but turned down or shipped out.

Dynamite ideas are well outside the boundary lines of the company way which involves steady, controlled progress and growth. As far as your company is concerned, it is always evolution, not revolution. That's the way it is for them. And you remember why the company way works. Don't you?

So save dynamite ideas for your own use. Find a backer. Or go for it on your own. And do it all yourself.

If you get a breakthrough idea that's really as good as you think it is, you deserve all the rewards anyway. And the payoff will be a lot richer than even a year or two of continuous 60-day raises.

It all goes back to what is needed and wanted at your company. And dynamite ideas seldom, if ever, are. Even companies as close to going under as the major American automakers have managed to successfully resist dynamite ideas about automotive engineering concepts. In their darkest days, they just keep turning out the same old slightly improved models.

For now, stay with the process of getting your raise. Changing your industry and changing the world can come later.

There is another side to the issue of getting personal at work. And now it's time to look at it. That other side involves, in part, the process of stepping back to create a wider context for personal relationships with everyone who works with you.

And in this expanded context, not one-on-one, but you and everyone you work with, getting personal is the ultimate long shot: the only one that never fails.

Here's how it works.

For most of us, the week is divided into time at home and time away from home.

Time at home focuses on you and your immediate family if you have one. It is introspective and inner-directed.

Time away from home focuses on everyone else. And the place where you work may well be your widest field of interaction with other people.

As such, time away from home creates the best opportunity you have to share yourself on a personal level as you really are and to contribute to a wide variety of other people's lives in a way that empowers them to go out and do the same.

The secret is that you, whoever you are, are wonderful just the way you are. You may not expresss yourself for fear of being evaluated, judged or put down. But whenever you don't hold back who you really are, everything will come to you. Including a lot of acknowledgment. And a lot of raises.

The problem is that there's a lot of stuff in the way of you expressing yourself as you really are. So what you express instead is a smaller, well-guarded, more hidden version of yourself. The more you withhold yourself that way, the more you shut down your life and the working environment around you.

That means, if you don't like the way your job is or the way your boss is, look and see how much of yourself you are putting in to your time at work each day. Then look and see how much of yourself you are hiding or withholding.

Do you want to get rid of some of the stuff that is suppressing you and everything about you that is truly wonderful right now? Do you want to start getting personal in a way that will support you and your co-workers? In style?

Use this page, or take out a piece of paper and, at the top, write a heading that says "What I don't want anyone to know about me is."

Then start listing everything you don't want anyone at work to ever find out about you. Be really specific and include everything that comes up. Don't leave out that overwhelming embarrassing thing, whatever it is. Yes, *that* thing.

Your list might include things like: The time you stole from your mother. A kinky sex experience. Dishonesty on your expense account or in handling company property or office supplies. An extramarital fling. A drug or alcohol problem. The time you wet your pants. Or whatever else.

Don't censor yourself. What you leave out will come between you and your capacity to truly express yourself.

What I don't want anyone to know about me is:

_____

_____

_____

_____

_____

Now, knowing what you have been hiding and making yourself wrong about and seeing it all in black and white, let all of that stuff go.

Just acknowledge it honestly and let it come to rest. If you find that hard to do, try forgiving yourself for it. Sometimes you may want to communicate something about an item on your list to one or two appropriate people to complete a part of your life that has been hanging around too long. You'll know if you need to do that or not.

The immediate result of this exercise is that you will notice your participation at work going up to new levels.

As you hide less because you are able to let old stuff go instead of carrying it around, everyone will notice you more. Including your boss. And rewards will follow automatically.

On a day-to-day level, being who you are involves many of the things you have been reading about. Saying "Good morning." Checking about someone else's coffee when you go to get your own. Supporting co-workers through personal problems, difficulties or other barriers.

And most of all, it involves being open and truthful with everyone at work instead of coming from old positions you may have had about competition and competitiveness.

Once you stop experiencing yourself as being separate or different from other people at work, you'll begin to lose the holding-back that goes along with the alienation of a Them-against-Me frame of reference.

Remember that it's never you against them anyway. Unless you say it is. And that the raise you'll get in 60 days does not come out of anyone else's pocketbook.

As you share more and more of yourself at work, you may notice that you have increased opportunities to be around the power source at your company.

The power source is the person who originates the work you do and who controls the finances that flow your way. That person is usually higher up the corporate ladder than your supervisor and may even be at the very top.

Getting to know and being around the power source at your company is not like cultivating a relationship with a company friend. A company friend is a long-range asset. The power source may generate immediate results.

Such as a raise in 60 days.

The way you get to be around the power source in your organization will happen spontaneously. It will be caused by your sharing yourself on a more and more meaningful level and really expressing who you are. If you *try* to get to know the power source at your company, it won't work.

You'll probably just be doing your job and the power source will approach you. He or she will say something conversational. And you'll have a chance to share something real or a chance to stiffen up and blow it.

If you choose not to blow it, say something spontaneous and genuine. Even if that means saying, "Oh boy, I really feel nervous talking to you. I've been hearing about you since I came to work here."

That way, you'll get what you wanted all along. Another opportunity to talk together another time.

That next time, your company homework will help. You can talk about the history of the company, if that's a favorite subject of the power source. Or ask about a problem you're running into in marathon training or golf or ballet or whatever interest you and the power source at your company may share outside of work.

Just being around your power source will generally make a difference.

One company president says, "I was sitting in my office last winter and a woman I remembered talking with in the data processing department came in. We started to talk and suddenly our chat turned into chattering. She started to shiver so badly, I couldn't understand a word she said.

"I always keep a window wide open, even in the dead of winter. And when she left, I realized that the January wind had gotten to her. On a sudden impulse, I called accounting and put through a raise for her. There was just something about her spirit that I liked.

"A couple of days later, I stopped at her desk and she thanked me for the raise. I asked her what it was that she had tried to tell me in my office and acknowledged that I hadn't understood a word of it.

"Was she surprised! It turned out that she had stopped in to ask me for more money!"

Just being there is all you have to do. Just being there. Being who you are. Without hiding out or holding back.

If you don't think that's enough, do this: Find out what the power source at your company hates doing most. And volunteer to do it for him or her as an additional function of your job.

Yes. It's the same thing you asked your immediate supervisor. And it's a good idea to have been doing that kind of extra work for your supervisor before you approach the power source. It doesn't look as if you are going over your immediate boss's head that way.

Taking over an unpleasant duty for the company power source can produce immediate results.

The head of a national recruitment firm tells exactly how powerfully it works. "I started the company myself and ran it all myself for a number of years. Then, as the company grew, I noticed how much I hated doing administrative work. One of the employees became aware of that and volunteered to assist me at it.

"He was so good at office administration that within a year I made him a full partner and put him in charge of all administrative activity.

"The next thing I liked doing least of all was cold-call telephoning for listings. A woman working as an interviewer offered to make cold calls for me for an hour a day and stay late if she needed to, just to make sure her regular job was handled.

"She turned out to be a terrific cold-caller. In fact, she produced double the results I was getting in about half the time. I made her a partner too, because of her contribution to the company's growth.

"The bottom line is that I actually gave away two-thirds of a really profitable operation. Just so I could do what I like doing best: developing new concepts for recruitment events and then producing them.

"With the business of running the company and taking care of details I hated to take care of all being managed so well by my partners, the two-thirds of the company I gave away was well worth it. And each of us now takes home more than twice what I used to when I managed everything myself."

That's what the positive side of getting personal can do for you.

By sharing yourself completely, on a personal level, you get noticed. You also get admired and acknowledged. And you invariably make a genuine impression on your co-workers, your supervisor and the power source at your company. You can learn about or literally create new opportunities for advancement out of unwanted aspects of your power source's job. You could even move into a partnership position. And if you don't want a partnership and the headaches that might go along with it, you will always have a spontaneous inside track to whatever it is that you do want from your company.

Including your next raise.

HOW TO GET MORE MONEY

- Avoid intimate relationships. They don't work.
- Don't leave your job for more money. That doesn't work either.

- Save dynamite ideas for your own use. They don't get you raises.
- Hide less and everyone will notice you more.
- Find a way to be around the power source at your company.

9

Nothing Succeeds Like Success Except Sometimes

The road to success is littered with the bodies of those who were seeking it.

Before you go for your raise in 60 days, which will be a sure sign of success, perhaps you had better take a look at who is responsible for all those bodies in the road.

Guess who?

"Last year, I hired two new people to sell our products over the telephone," says the sales manager of a large corporation. "Both of them agreed to work for a pretty good commission. And to make it more interesting, I set things up so each one could earn a $500 a week bonus on top of commissions for every five sales made during that week.

"One of them made three sales her first day and left her job on the second day. She saw how easy it would be to win. And she got scared.

"The other one kept coming back. But each week, he never made more than four sales. He always stopped one short of the bonus. His leads had a funny way of just falling through the cracks.

"After a while, he started to resent everything and said he deserved a bonus for every five sales, regardless of which week he produced them in.

"He started coming in late and leaving at five o'clock on the button. He took longer and longer lunches. He complained a lot.

"He stayed almost a year, averaging three or four sales a week. Hardly ever passing the bonus mark of five.

"Now any salesperson knows that if he was good enough to sell consistently at that level, he could have made twenty or thirty sales a week and really cashed in. Instead, he chose to live grudgingly on adequate but certainly not extravagant commission checks.

"I gave both people total control of their incomes. Neither one could handle it."

A lot of us are like that.

Some kind of built-in boobytrap always keeps blowing up, right in the face of success. And then, BAM! Another body in the road.

"I just spent the weekend with a couple I've known since college," says the president of a chain of retail specialty stores. "The woman has been working for just under a year. And what she was telling me reminds me of my own employees' stories.

"To get a raise, she needs to move up to the next classification. She's positive that her supervisor won't support her. She calls him chauvinistic and narrow-minded.

"She told me her only other option is to transfer to one of two other divisions. But she says she can't do that because all the other people in those divisions have higher degrees than she does. That's not a company barrier, by the way. That's her mind chattering at her.

"She said she couldn't talk with the division manager because he doesn't have the time. And she can't write him a memo because he'd never read it.

"She's even got reasons why she can't enroll her husband's assistance. He works for the same company. In fact, he's the personnel manager there. And he could easily quarterback the move up and the raise that goes with it.

"She's typical of all the people who work for me who aren't asking for or getting raises for reasons all their own. They tell themselves the economy's bad. Or they're earning more than other people in their community.

"They have all these stories.

"And their stories come between them and their raises. I don't even have to say 'No'. They say 'No' for me and then they even make up stories and reasons to justify and validate it to themselves.

"If they'd give up their stories they'd see that nothing is standing in the way of their raises.

"Except themselves."

Fear of success. Negative beliefs about success. Thoughts and stories and reasons why success is not attainable. They're all part of the same pattern.

Do you want to see your own version of it?

Turn to page 100. Or take out a blank piece of paper and write a heading at the top that says "The bad thing about succeeding is."

Then write down all the bad things that come to mind. Stay with it until you have at least ten or fifteen bad things about succeeding listed and you are sure you haven't left anything out. Include bad things like pride going before a fall, other people being envious and not liking you anymore, higher taxes to pay and whatever else applies to you.

The bad thing about succeeding is:

_____

_____

_____

_____

_____

_____

_____

_____

_____

_____

_____

You may be surprised at what you come up with if you really let go and get involved in your list.

It will be a pattern of failure or of penny-ante success that you have always had. One that you can't afford to continue any longer.

The way to break up the pattern is simply to notice that you have it. And to become fully conscious about those times when you quietly and compulsively fall into it.

The fact is most people are more afraid of succeeding than they are of failing. And maybe, without fully knowing it, you have been one of them. Until now.

Failing is safe. It is even comfortable because you can always blame it on someone or something else.

Failing is easy. You are never responsible for what happens. It is always the circumstances that do it to you. It is because of your parents or your age or your lack of education or your overqualification in education or your race or your gender or your religion or your bad back or your toilet training. It is easy to blame all that stuff when something goes wrong.

And conversely, when something good happens, it is always luck. Or an accident.

The reason for this widespread fear of success is that succeeding is a universal acknowledgment of how tremendously powerful you really are.

Once you open up to the idea that you can choose to have it any way you want it and that it is well within your power to have your life work and your income work, it becomes increasingly difficult for you to blame other people or other circumstances for what happens ever again.

Then you can begin to look at failure a whole new way.

Failure only represents a lack of something in your life that you thought you needed to have in order to be all right. As a result, whenever you fail, you try and try to succeed in order to prove that you are really all right or okay or a successful person. That's what robs you of success.

The more you try to change failure, the more you resist your experience of failing. And the more stuck you get as more and more failure sticks around.

Want to see failure fade away fast?

Choose to fail.

Really get into the experience of choosing it. And notice what it feels like. Where it shows up in your body. What color it would be if it had a color. How big it would be if it had a size. How much it would weigh if it had weight.

Choose to fail. Experience it. And watch what happens.

Whenever you choose to want what you have, you haven't failed. You have succeeded.

You may be confusing the difference between failure and having problems you associate with failure. Problems like not enough money. Not enough approval or acknowledgment. No car or place to live. And all that stuff.

Failing and having problems are not the same. They are never the same.

Everything has problems.

Billionaires have problems. TV stars have problems. Dentists have problems. The good life has lots of problems. A new car has problems. You have problems.

Do you know who is responsible for *your* problems?

That's right. Too bad again. You can't blame anyone else.

You create your own problems to give yourself the opportunities to expand your life. And then you create more problems to expand more. And more problems to expand more. And even more problems to expand even more.

Problems are like growth rings in a tree. They take you to the next level of your life. Whenever you can play with problems, your experience of life will take on a new dimension altogether.

Re-reading Chapter 4 and reviewing the exercises you did will give you a quick refresher course on what money problems are all about.

Notice who is the source of all the problems in your life. Just notice. That's all.

Can you take complete responsibility for what you notice?

If you still have any doubt about the issue of problems, I want you to stop reading for a few minutes. And recall a few of any major problems you have had recently or in the past.

Now notice the one element that is always there whenever a problem is happening in your life. If you see that it is you who is always around whenever you're having a problem, you are absolutely right.

The prize is that you can now begin to handle success.

So start right here. By getting clear about what success really is. Success is always a goal. It is never an end in itself. Each goal that you achieve moves you further along the path of your intentions. And that path never ends.

The end result of achieving a goal or succeeding has to always be the beginning of the next step along whatever path you have chosen to follow.

Once you have mastered that, your goals produce miraculous results. All by themselves.

Satisfaction from success only lasts as long as you are willing to keep moving on to whatever's next.

Success is always another step. It's a step on a stairway to another goal and never simply having something that's different or better than what you have now.

As far as this book is concerned, success means getting a raise. It's the raise you intended to get when you set up your Get A Raise Game back in Chapter 3.

The final point to cover about success is the ethics involved in succeeding. And if your list about "The bad thing about succeeding" includes anything like "You lose all your friends" or "Nice guys finish last," this part is for you.

Whatever ethical system you follow or endorse needs to be very carefully examined within the context of Your Get A Raise Game. Chances are, that ethical system will come out perfectly all right.

If you have followed the Raise Game guidelines I suggested, you'll keep noticing the following things.

Your game is not competitive. You are not engaging in a struggle to take a raise away from anyone else. No one else has even been invited to play your game with you or against you. You are simply getting a raise. Your raise. And it is quite possible that your raise will create other raises for other people with similar jobs at work. Which means it could turn out to be good for you and them instead of something that was only good for you or them. That is certainly not competitive.

Your game is not selfish or greedy. You are not after more than your share. The concept of a share in a single pie doesn't even hold up. Your raise is not bad or wrong. It is simply a raise. Your raise. And later on, after you get it, you can share it with anyone else you'd like. That's up to you. And that definitely is not selfish or greedy.

Your game is not manipulative, sneaky or conniving. You won't be doing anything that is furtive or covert. Everything you do will be out in the open and larger than life so everyone can see it, notice it, and reward you appropriately for it. You will be openly and honestly getting a raise. Your raise.

Most ethical systems have a tendency to package a lot of judgments and evaluations into something about the size of a small candle dripping. And then apply that to the whole ball of wax.

It is often advisable to unravel that package even though it seems small and tidy and tightly packed. Then if you have to, you can make your own judgments and evaluations.

When you do, you'll see that success and money are never right or wrong. It is using them appropriately or inappropriately that may be right or wrong.

But even better than making your own judgments and evaluations is not making any judgments or evaluations at all.

That's somewhat hard to do. Especially at first. And it's worth looking at.

When you come from a framework that clear and clean, your ideas about success and money can include using them appropriately and inappropriately with equal weight and equal emphasis. You'll see that neither is intrinsically right or wrong. One may simply be more workable than the other.

And from there, it's just a quick jump to what may be the most valid ethical base for success of all:

What's good is whatever produces the greatest amount of aliveness.

That really works. Because you will never feel truly alive if you achieve success competitively, selfishly, greedily, manipulatively, sneakily or connivingly. There will be a dead spot inside of you associated with what you did. And it will grow, deadening everything else as it spreads.

You will feel truly alive if you play your Get A Raise Game flat-out and win at it. And then if you use your new level of successfully achieving your goal as the basis for your next step out.

Now that you have moved through some serious stuff about success, playing is the next order of the day. What you will be playing and winning is the game you created: the game called Get A Raise in 60 Days.

HOW TO GET MORE MONEY

- Be aware of how much more afraid you are of success than of failure.
- Notice who is responsible for your failures. Then remember, if you choose to fail, it's not failure, it's what you chose. Choose to succeed.
- Remember that satisfaction from success only lasts as long as you keep moving on to your next goal.

10

Get Your Raise
in 60 Days

So the big moment is here. And you are going to start the 60-day period of your Get A Raise Game and get your raise.

Are you really clear about what your Get A Raise Game is all about?

Getting your raise is a really serious matter. And, as you've seen, if you go at it as if it were life-and-death or struggle-and-effort, it's going to be really hard to get.

Instead, you are going to play a Raise Game and make it easier and much more enjoyable to get your raise.

Use the following form to cast your own Get A Raise Game in concrete terms right now. Before you read any further.

By the way, if you are one of those people who turned to this chapter to read first, I want you to know that this chapter won't work unless you first create the foundation, context and space for it to work. To do that, you have to read each chapter in sequence and go through the exercises that enable you to be successful at materializing your goals.

MY GET A RAISE GAME

1. Setting up the game:

   Whose game is it?   ( ) Mine   ( ) Someone else's
   Whose raise will it be?   ( ) Mine   ( ) Someone else's
   Who says how I win?   ( ) I do   ( ) Someone else does

2. Setting up the rules:

   How long will the game last?
   ( ) 60 days   ( ) Some other length of time _____
   How large a raise do I have to get to win?
   _____   by   _____
   Bottom line figure   Bottom line date
   How large a raise do I have to get to win big?
   How fast do I have to get it?
   _____   by   _____
   Go-for-it figure   Go-for-it date
   How flat-out am I willing to play?
   ( ) 100%   ( ) Some other percent _____
     Do I really want to play at all?   ( ) Yes   ( ) No
   Whose rules are these?
   ( ) My rules   ( ) Someone else's rules

3. Checking out the rules:

   Is my game too easy?   ( ) Yes   ( ) No
   Is my game too hard?   ( ) Yes   ( ) No

4. Checking out yourself:

   Can I live with my rules?   ( ) Yes   ( ) No
   Am I willing to follow my rules?   ( ) Yes   ( ) No
   Am I willing to take complete responsibility for the creation of this game and its outcome?
   ( ) Yes   ( ) No

Am I still willing to play flat-out 100 percent for the entire period of the game?
( ) Yes   ( ) No

Am I willing to use all my resources and include all my stuff?
( ) Yes   ( ) No

For the full period of the game, am I willing to let go of all considerations about how much I need a raise, want a raise, deserve a raise or feel entitled to a raise?
( ) Yes   ( ) No

Have I fully identified my negative beliefs and thoughts about money and success so that I can include them in my game as obstacles but not get stuck in them?
( ) Yes   ( ) No
(If you haven't, reread Chapters 5 and 9 right away.)

5. Declare yourself:

I will tell the following ten people about my intention to create a $_____ raise in the next ____ days.

1. _____	6. _____
2. _____	7. _____
3. _____	8. _____
4. _____	9. _____
5. _____	10. _____

I will also tell the following ten people about my intention to create a $_____ raise in the next ____ days.

1. _____	6. _____
2. _____	7. _____
3. _____	8. _____
4. _____	9. _____
5. _____	10. _____

I realize that if I take responsibility for keeping my word and sticking to my game that I will get a raise and if I don't, I won't.

_____
Sign here

Now that you have written out your Get A Raise game plan, you may have noticed how simple a game plan it is.

Getting what you want in life needs to always be that simple. And easy. And challenging. And fun. And worthy of being played at a 100 percent level.

You see, if getting a raise had to be as serious and heavy and depressing as it used to be, you'd just keep getting the same results you used to get. And you know what they were.

This is a new game. With new, fast, high-level results. And that's strictly because it is a game and because you say you are willing to play it.

So for the last time, keep remembering that it is just a game. And that it is definitely not about needing the money really badly because your rent's going up, your car's falling apart, your kid needs braces, your cello just cracked and your cat is pregnant. All those things may be true, but none of them have anything to do with your Get A Raise Game.

Your Get A Raise Game is only about getting a raise. You need to focus on the raise and on the joy and excitement of getting it, not on any external matters. Those will just get in your way.

OK?

OK.

Here's an example of how getting a raise for its own sake works.

A communications specialist told me about her first job at a major New York advertising agency: "I was supposed to start at $14,000 but someone made a mistake on the form. My paychecks looked a little larger than I had expected, but who knows from numbers? I work with words and visual ideas.

"After I had been there for four months, my boss called me into his office and told me he had filled out my salary form wrong. As a result, I was getting paid $21,000 a year instead of $14,000.

"I told him 'Wait a minute! You're not going to take that back, are you? Not after I've gotten used to having it!'

"He agreed that my performance was certainly worth being paid at that level and said he'd let my salary stand the way it was.

"On an impulse and for no reason at all, I pointed out that I had been working there for almost half a year and that I wanted a raise.

"I just happened to have under my arm a new ad campaign I was working on and I showed it to him.

"He must have liked it. I got another $7000 raise. Which made me an honest $14,000 a year richer in less than five minutes!"

Notice: No problems. No need. No life-and-death qualities. No epic struggle.

Just a $14,000 raise.

Just because.

Here is what to do to get your own raise. From the first day of your Get A Raise Game through the sixtieth.

Enroll your supervisor's support. Get him or her to participate in your game with you.

On the first day, walk in and say something like "I've come to the conclusion that I want to work more effectively for you. I want my job to be more enlivening and I want to produce significant results. I am also committed to supporting you in your job and seeing to it that you look really good around here. I'm willing to play full tilt to do all that and I want to know exactly what you think I need to do. And, by the way, when I start producing those results, how long do you think it will take me to get a raise?"

That puts your game in motion.

Then stop in to see your supervisor at least once a week. Ask how you're doing. Find out what duties your supervisor hates doing most so that you can volunteer to take them over and do them yourself.

Use the opportunity of increased contact with your supervisor to make sure you know what your own basic job specifications are. Remember, you will get a raise for doing what you were hired to do if you do it as well as it can be done.

Find out what is needed and wanted. By your company on an over-all level. By your department. By your supervisor. By whichever power source approves your salary hikes. Make it your job to provide whatever that is. For all of them.

Keep your attention focused on what they need and want and you will avoid getting bogged down in your own problems and positions about whatever you used to think *you* wanted and needed. And you'll get *your* raise.

Cultivate the grapevine. You will learn invaluable information about trends, current company goals and personal issues that may open up opportunities to be of sevice in needed and wanted areas.

Don't get hooked by rumors. Just keep your eyes and ears open. Become aware and more conscious about **every**thing that is going on around you at work than you have ever been before.

Seek out company friends at all levels. It never hurts to have teachers or guides and a mentor on your side. People willing to fill those roles are all around you. Each one can become a key source of data about corporate and individual needs and wants. Each one is another link in the chain that will lead you to your raise.

Research, research, research. Clip articles about your company or your field of work and start a file folder to keep them in. Buy a book about a work-related subject without asking for or expecting reimbursement. Go to the library and find out what's new in your type of work. Read your company's latest annual report and newsletter and get an idea of where the next step is. That way, you'll be there waiting when everyone else drives up later in the company car.

Here is what this kind of research did for one person and can do for you.

"Ten years ago, I was working for a steel mill as an industrial engineer. My job included a bi-weekly regression analysis and correlation report in which two kinds of data were run off manually on a desktop calculator. It took sixteen hours to complete this single step. And it was the most boring work I have ever done.

"Since we had a computer, I suggested to my supervisor that a program be developed to perform the task. But month after month, priorities kept getting in the way.

"After three more months of boredom, I bought a few books about Fortran and spent my evenings writing my own software package. After another couple of months of development, I submitted my homegrown program to management for a test run.

"The tedious sixteen-hour job was reduced to one and a half hours of data entry and processing time. Within six weeks, I was given a 30 percent raise.

"And less than four months later, my reputation as a data processing expert led to a promotion to Division Systems Analyst with still another 30 percent raise."

That's only the beginning. Here's what else to do while you are playing your Get A Raise Game at a 100 percent level.

Share yourself always and in all ways. Say "Good morning" and "Good night" to everyone you see. Bring a few doughnuts in once in a while. Support people around you. Spread your enthusiasm as if there were no tomorrow.

Most of all, avoid meaningless conversations and small talk about the weather, the ballgame or the bad coffee.

Instead, whenever it's appropriate, express something unique and wonderful about yourself.

Miracles happen to you every day. Share them. You find a quarter. You see a high school sweetheart in the street. Your hamster dies. You finally communicate lovingly with your teenage son. All miracles. And all of that is much more inspiring and enlivening stuff than talk about the weather or last night's television shows.

Share your miracles and watch other people open up.

Become more visible. The more people at your company know who you are, the more likely you are to be remembered and rewarded.

How do you make yourself more visible? Promote yourself shamelessly. Do it just as if you were your own public relations agent.

Write memos. Even while you are checking in regularly with your boss, write short memos that summarize what you have been producing in the way of results. When it comes to effective self-promotion, a two-paragraph memo is worth a two-hour review of your progress.

Be active at trade shows. Or union meetings. Or outside work-related areas. When competitors are impressed with you, word always gets back to your boss. Becoming more visible outside of your company has the effect of making you more visible inside as well.

Seek speaking engagements. Trade and professional groups are perfect places to promote yourself and to be seen favorably as a representative of your company. Definitely tell your supervisor and management people when you have been invited to speak at any of these gatherings.

Do whatever it takes to be noticed positively. Write a feature for the company newspaper or house organ. Handle collections for the United Fund or a new baby shower. Higher visibility comes in lots of forms. Be creative and come up with as many as you can, every week.

Get outside acknowledgment for your work. Local newspapers and business or industry publications are always hungry for new material. Make yourself available to people who work for these publications. If you are quoted a few times, you will soon become a regular spokesperson. And, people in your company are sure to notice. However, this technique is not applicable to everybody and you must be careful not to upstage your boss.

Check in with secretaries. Be friendly and cordial. Also be sure that they are aware of your good work and increased effectiveness. Their bosses will hear about you from them. Secondhand self-promotion works just as well as doing it yourself.

Other areas at work will intersect with these high visibility ones and create the complete framework for your raise. In fact, no one thing can materialize your raise all by itself. It takes a combination of ingredients.

So, be sure to include the following:

Plug yourself into your power source. Find out who gets the final vote on your raise and connect with him or her. You can use any of the ways suggested in Chapter 5. Or come up with a few new ones of your own.

If you can do something directly for your power source that he or she would rather not do or hates to do, you can almost start counting the extra dollars each week.

Use your company raise system. Or don't. But never make it wrong. If your corporation's policy calls for raise-reviews every six or twelve months, be willing to give up that raise to get the one you will get in 60 days. You can always play another Get A Raise Game and go for it again in another two or three months. Or whenever you like.

You can include a promotion with your raise if you would like one or if that is the only way you think you can break free of the established system. Naturally, that's not the only way. No one way is ever the only way unless you say it is.

"My own system usually involves taking on another responsibility that includes work outside of the office," says a corporate executive. "Of course, I need a company car to handle the work.

"So I get the car and the expense account that goes with it. When the work I volunteered to do is completed some two or three months later and they want the car back, I tell them that it's an extra benefit worth income and I negotiate for the difference.

"At review time when they tell me I just got a raise, I point out that what I got wasn't a raise. It was a settlement to make up for a lost fringe benefit.

"Nine times out of ten, I've gotten a raise on top of it."

Another way to use the company review system is to look for loopholes and cash in on them. "When a new salary administration system was installed this year at our company," says a petroleum company supervisor, "one of our people who had recently been promoted to a new job category from a very low salary-base received an automatic adjustment in the form of a $6000 raise.

"Was she shocked! All she had expected was $1000." So be sure to examine all new salary structures carefully and be certain that you have gotten everything you deserve.

Still another way to use the company review system is to choose not to use it at all. Just realize that your Get A Raise Game can include the company system along with all the other stuff, but that it doesn't have to involve it, activate it or tangle with it in any way.

The idea is not to go along with any notions that include your being confined by a system that's not an intrinsic part of your game.

You never have to be trapped by anything. Unless you choose to be.

Keep your agreements. Keep those agreements you made back in Chapter 6 about getting your work to work. In fact, keep the list or a copy of it with you for the 60 days of your Get A Raise Game. And make it a point to look it over once a day to remind yourself all about how large a game you have chosen to play.

Find and use new resources. Things about yourself that you may have overlooked can qualify you for unexpected raises.

For instance, your interest in graphic arts, electronics, marketing, union relations or video games may qualify you for education funds from your company with the promise of a raise or a better position when you complete your course.

Give up the idea that you have anything to lose. You don't. When you do things for the company, learn to remain emotionally detached. That way, you will do for them what you might not ever do for yourself because of your fear of rejection or some other personal stuff.

"I recently asked one of the people here to make a call for me to find out what a new copy machine would cost," says the manager of a small office.

"Instead of just that one call, she telephoned two competing copy machine companies. Reporting back the results, she told me about a high degree of competitiveness about price. She asked whether I'd like her to let the companies face off.

"I gave her the OK.

"Over the next five days she negotiated with both companies for me. The final price was less than half of one of the original quotes.

"No one asked her to do that. And she said she would never have had the patience or determination to do it for herself. But in this case, it got to be interesting for her because she had nothing to lose and nothing personal at stake.

"It turned out she had a lot to gain. One week later, I made sure that her paycheck included a substantial raise."

Everything you have read so far in this chapter shows what it means to play your Get A Raise Game at a 100 percent level.

It may sound like a lot to do.

It's not.

Whenever you play flat-out and don't hold back or save any energy for next time, you'll be amazed at how much you can accomplish in the framework of just doing your job.

One more thing.

While you are doing everything else, do this:

As you do your job for the next 60 days, do it as if you have already reached the next salary level that you intend to reach.

If you are making $5.50 an hour and you want to make $6 an hour, do your $5.50-an-hour job the way a $6-an-hour employee would do it. With the same ease, the same expertise, the same professionalism and the same attention to detail.

If you are earning $20,000 a year and you want to earn $30,000, do your $20,000-a-year job the way someone who was making $30,000 a year would do it. With the same ease, the same expertise, the same professionalism and the same attention to detail.

Act and perform as if you have already received the raise you intend to get. And keep it up for the entire period of your Get A Raise Game.

It's just like a follow-through swing in golf or tennis, a basketball shot or a karate chop.

In each case, you make sure the action is done correctly by physically moving past the point where the ball is hit or the brick is broken or the raise is given. Then the action completes itself. All by itself.

Your full attention is on whatever happens after the result is produced. Instead of the result itself. And there is absolutely no way you can trip yourself up.

Do the job of a person who has already earned the raise you intend to have for only 60 days and that raise is as good as yours.

As you will soon see for yourself.

HOW TO GET MORE MONEY

- Make getting the raise you want simple, challenging and fun.
- Get your supervisor's help in your Get A Raise Game.
- Do your job as if you've already gotten your raise.
- Be open and friendly.
- Expect miracles to happen for you every day. Share them with your co-workers instead of making small talk.
- Keep your list of agreements with you at all times. And stick to them.

11

The Final Confrontation

Let's pretend you have been playing your Get A Raise Game
for almost 60 days. And you've played it flat-out at a 100
percent capacity. Just as you said you would.

All that time, it didn't matter how you felt or what
thoughts you may have had or what may have happened in
response or reaction to your game. Nothing has diminished
your willingness to play as if there were no tomorrow.

And you've done everything you read about in Chapter
10. In fact, you really got into the spirit of the game and came
up with a few of your own extra-special ways to play.

And you have really made a noticeable and distinct
contribution. You found a way to get something done that
the company needed and wanted done. You even set things
up so that you could receive the credit and the
acknowledgment instead of letting it slip away.

And you've handled the job you were hired to do at the
same time. With all the care, precision and consciousness of
an orbiting astronaut or a brain surgeon. You have certainly

handled it at the next-highest level of salary that you targeted for your raise.

Well, let's pretend that the time is up now. It's been almost 60 days. So you're ready to check out the results you said you would produce and see how well you produced them.

One of two things happened.

You got the raise.

Or you didn't get the raise.

If you got the raise, go directly to the next chapter. If you didn't get the raise, read on.

Not getting the raise when the game is over or almost over doesn't mean you didn't get the raise.

It might just mean that you didn't get the raise *yet*.

And if you get past the fifty-fourth day of your game and you do not have your raise yet, playing flat-out involves keeping your intention up, keeping your game in motion and, in addition, one last step: Confronting your boss.

Confronting your boss might mean meeting with your immediate supervisor. Or getting a discussion group together that includes your supervisor, your department head and the vice-president or management person in charge of your department head. Or any combination of people in between.

Your research and company friends will have told you how the company hierarchy affects your raise. So you know who needs to be booked for a meeting or a series of meetings about your raise.

Use your judgment about formality. At many companies a simple informal approach works best. Instead of setting up a conference for next Friday at 3:15, you might want to just walk in and simply say, "I want to talk to you."

Usually the response will be, "About what?"

And just as simply, you can say "About money."

Be really sure you have chosen a moment when your boss can be fully available to listen to you. If she has a board meeting in twenty minutes or he's had a three-martini lunch or a root-canal excavation or your company's stock just dropped forty-seven points, another moment on another day might be better.

When you sense the time is right, jump in with both feet moving.

Communication style will become extremely important at this point. And it will be your responsibility to present yourself in a way that guarantees your boss will both hear you and get your messge.

If you've never been an effective speaker and especially if you tend to let your feelings and judgments come between you and the content of what you want to say, a few basic guidelines will give you a new sense of self-confidence and ease.

Clear yourself by becoming aware of all your stuff before you begin. Notice whether you are feeling scared or unconscious or angry. And don't act out any role that doesn't support you. For instance, a nice-little-boy act or a wronged-women act or a deserving martyr act won't work right now. Simply file it away with your other stuff. After you acknowledge it to yourself, it will never get in your way.

Don't try to change your emotions. And don't pretend you don't have any emotions. Just let them be the way they are. And keep reminding yourself what your purpose is. And then choose to stick with that.

Breathe deeply. Whenever you notice that you're feeling tense or defensive or anything else that seems counterproductive, pause. Then take a long, slow, deep breath.

Don't talk in generalities or abstractions. Be specific. Use simple words that are easy to understand and identify with. And keep restating your basic message. It doesn't matter how many times you say it.

Listen carefully when your boss is speaking. Considerations about your raise are certain to come up. And the way to handle considerations is to not resist them, to acknowledge them without agreeing with them and then to restate your message.

Like this.

"I want a raise." (Make it a simple statement, not a declaration or demand.)

"Well, the economy is in bad shape right now and money is really tight around here."

"That's true. Money seems really tight and the economy is way off. And I want a raise."

"Let's see, your review period doesn't come up for another four months."

"No, it doesn't. I've been doing an exceptional job around here and producing results (list one or two quickly). And I want a raise."

"Your department has been one of the lowest profit centers around here. There are no raises in the budget for any of you."

"Yes, I know my department has had problems. I have a couple of ideas that might turn that around. For instance, (list a few). I am making myself responsible for the smooth operation of my department. And I want a raise."

"I don't think I can justify a raise for you unless I give raises to everyone else too."

"My raise might be hard to justify. On the other hand, it might inspire everyone else to work harder and be more productive, as I have been doing. I really want a raise."

"OK."

Notice the simplicity and directness of the flow. You never get defensive. You never agree with your boss's problems in a way that adds weight to them. You follow each consideration completely without adding your own resistance to it.

And if any single obstacle keeps coming up, just keep processing it over and over the same way until it dissolves. It's as easy to do in real life as it seems in the hypothetical confrontation you just read. Repeat each reason or argument against your raise that your boss presents. This shows that you are paying attention. Then without being defensive, point out why that reason or argument, as valid as it is, does not apply to your request.

Eventually you get what you want.

Why?

Because for the last 60 days, you have been doing the world's greatest job for your company. You have been making a major contribution. You have turned your entire image around. You've even been pleasant and fun to have around because you've been playing a game instead of being involved in a life-and-death struggle for survival.

Your boss would have to be crazy not to see value in all that.

So your boss wants to give you your raise. Your boss really does. His or her desire to reward you is clearly there on the bottom line. And your boss also has considerations about giving you your raise.

At this point, therefore, it becomes your job to press your boss through all the considerations that come between him and doing what he really wants to do. Or to support her through her conflicting thoughts or imagined problems about your raise and keep her playing your game with you.

Considerations, obstacles, thoughts and imagined problems disappear like mist when you don't resist them and add weight to them.

And on top of that, the generosity with which you have been sharing yourself at work will now begin to come back to you. With dollar signs attached.

"It gets down to an employee's willingness to give that determines raises," says the president of an athletic shoe company. "The more you give, the more you get back. Withholders lose out and footdraggers don't get raises.

"A woman came to work here as a part-time receptionist and got three raises in less than six months. She moved up from $7000 a year to become our advertising manager at $22,000 within that time.

"She was more in touch with her intention than anyone I've ever seen. Whatever we gave her to do got done, along with anything else that came up. And she was always in my office looking for feedback.

"She was the most generous person I've ever worked with, always interested in giving. She was so generous that she had no qualms about holding me up for money.

"She knew her worth and wouldn't settle for less. She actually made herself the most valuable person in the company. And then acted that way.

"It's a willingness to give, balanced by a willingness to take back, reinforced by a willingness to give even more. As a result, she was always feeling good about herself. And so was everyone else.

"Her one problem was not liking to do the same job for more than three or four months. So the end of the story is that she went to work for our advertising agency at double her salary here.

"One year out of college, she is the account supervisor on my business, with the kind of job diversity and financial benefit package most people would kill for.

"The point is, she couldn't have gotten there by killing. It was all a result of giving."

Did you get all that?

Check yourself out on the key area:

How do you handle your relationship with your boss? Do you feel small and powerless or covertly hostile and aggressive? Or do you feel supremely confident of your worth to the company as an individual?

Finally, are you willing to ask for your raise? Without forcing the issue? Simply and directly?

After you create all the other conditions for getting your raise, the final condition is stepping past all your internal barriers to expresing yourself and asking for what you want. Losing out in life is more a result of holding back at this single point that anything else.

Another factor involves the amount of your raise. The bottom line you targeted for is your minimum acceptable amount. Right?

Sometimes the amount of your raise can be built into your confrontation talks. But frequently it becomes a separate issue.

Whichever it is, remember this: It's still your game. Keep playing.

That means, don't shut down.

Maintain your intention persistently and as assertively as you can by saying "I want a raise" or "I want a $5000 raise" or "I want a $2.25-an-hour raise" as many times as it takes to get past your boss's considerations, excuses or counter arguments.

You may choose to ask for a higher raise than your bottom-line figure if you think you'll have to negotiate. Just keep remembering who set up the bottom line in the first place and who said that's what it would take to win the game.

Avoid becoming caught up in your own emotional reactions and responses by noticing each one as it comes up, breathing deeply and letting it be there just the way it is. If you don't try to resist an emotion or change an emotion for a better or different emotion or act out an emotion, it will never become a problem.

And when you sense that you have gone as far as you can go, suggest a workable compromise. It doesn't have to be the best raise. It has to be the raise you can live with. And even then, the outcome may not be fully resolved at that meeting.

Here is what it means never to give up your power to create what you intend to have.

The financial vice-president of a large textile corporation tells about the time she told one of her accounting people to add a $25-a-week raise to his salary. "After five or six weeks, I found a bookkeeping discrepancy and traced it to that employee's raise. He had not been taking it. So the payroll books didn't balance.

"When I called him in and asked why, he told me that $25 a week wasn't enough of a raise and that his contributions to the company were worth at least three times more than that.

"After I stopped feeling angry and defensive, I realized first that he was right. And second, that during the past five or six weeks while he had been rejecting an inadequate raise, his work continued to be at just as high a level as always. He had made his statement by turning down a raise. Not by expresssing anger, discontent, depression or smallness in his work.

"The $75-a-week raise he got was given retroactively. It was worth it!"

Other issues occasionally come up. All of which you can now begin to handle with more and more effectiveness.

For example, as I write this, I've become aware that many companies are freezing wages because of current economic conditions. If you find your Get A Raise Game being played out against a wage freeze, keep playing it out. Confront the situation head-on with your boss. And get your raise retroactively after the melt. Or get yourself promoted to a new and unfrozen category.

By now, I'm sure you get the idea. And the idea is, you always have an unlimited number of options and which option to use is always up to you.

The last issue about your final confrontation with your boss is a fairly simple one.

According to the ground rules of your Raise Game, your raise will come from totally active participation at your company and within the framework of your job.

That means you can't play your game and, at the same time, hedge your bet by getting another job during game time and then using your new job as a club to beat a raise out of your current boss.

Counter-offer raises came up in Chapter 8 as an example of long shots that don't work. They never work because they are never built on a foundation of trust, openness, commitment to and involvement in your job. Looking for a counter-offer stops you from doing the best possible job in your current position. Job hunting is itself an all-consuming job that takes 100 percent of your effort. There's no way you can give 100 percent to two different jobs. And getting out never makes things better. You will probably face the same problems in your new job.

All that another job offer does is make it virtually impossible to create the kind of satisfaction it takes to get your raise the 60-day way.

You see, whenever it looks as if the grass is greener somewhere else or that something you don't have is better than whatever you do have, your life begins to take a one-way roller coaster to the bottom.

So don't make the mistake of thinking that you can win big by looking outside of whatever you are until you have made your work agreements, kept them, set up your Raise Game and played it all out full tilt.

Then and only then will you know whether you need to get another job or not.

It all becomes clear within the context of your game.

You see, if you stick to your rules and do what you say you'll do and you don't get a raise in 60 days, you will know once and for all that the job you have is not for you.

If you work where you are not acknowledged for your outstanding performance on the job, your sharing of who you really are and your total participation in a warm, personal and thoroughly giving manner, get out.

If you work where you come in ready to set new world records for whatever you do every day and no one supports you and encourages you, get out.

If you work where no matter what you do, you can't enjoy yourself and create an enlivening and challenging atmosphere, get out

There is no reason to hold back and waste your time, your enthusiasm and your life. Not when you are willing and able to play as big a game as the one you've been playing. And not when so many employers out there have had to put up with employees who hate their jobs. They would love to have someone like you who is willing to commit yourself to your job. Most employer's doors are always open to aliveness.

And that is true regardless of recessions, slowdowns and all other economic circumstances.

So now you can find out whether or not your company is the company for you. In just 60 days. Instead of hanging around being unsure and miserable for five, ten or twenty years.

Ninety-eight times out of one hundred, you are already in the right place. And this is the way to prove it.

It gives your Raise Game another dimension that way. And actually sets it up so that there is no way for you to lose.

Knowing that, you can relax about the outcome and stick to your intended game plan.

And get your raise in 60 days.

HOW TO GET MORE MONEY

- Confront your boss only when everything else has failed.

- Overcome your boss's objections, arguments and considerations by acknowledging them and then restating your request for a raise clearly and directly.

- Keep playing your game and keep your intention on getting your raise.

12
You Got It

A really terrific raise in 60 days.

Now you know how to get one.

Because now you know the key to it all has always been the one thing you have been the least willing to use on your job.

Your self.

Ever since the first chapter when you began to see the way it works, you've been creating a framework based on the simplest of principles:

When you put all of you, your whole self, into your job, you get back all that is there for you to get. But when you hold back and save some of you for the next time or the next job, they hold back and save some of their resources for the next raise period or the next employee.

There is no in-between.

It's either you *and* them in a partnership where you find out what they need and want and you provide it. And everyone wins.

Or it's you *or* them in a power struggle for the upper hand, for dominance and for being right.

And where there is no partnership, there are no winners. Everyone loses.

Knowing that, you can make your choice. And you can get your raise. Easily.

But one final word of warning. Your life will begin to work on a much higher level while you are in the process of getting your raise. And it will have nothing at all to do with getting the raise.

What it's all about is your willingness to just get there and play. You know, as long as you're doing your job all those hours every day, wouldn't you rather be having a good time at it?

Raises will come automatically with increasing frequency as your game at work keeps getting bigger and bigger.

So if you don't remember anything else, remember this: The minute you get your raise, don't stop. Don't put your feet up. Start a new game immediately.

The paradox is that it was never about winning. It has always been about the game itself.

If you don't remember that, watch out!

You will find yourself in the same old rut that had you looking for a raise and needing a raise in the first place. Your stuff about your job will get heavier and heavier again. You will develop some kind of conflict with your boss again. You will start showing up for work feeling angry or tense or depressed or sick again.

And none of that is really the way you want it to be anymore. Is it?

I mean, now that you know how to create what you want by letting your intention be bigger than circumstances or competition or anything else, you have the opportunity to turn this raise into another raise in 60 days. And another raise in 60 days after that.

All you have to do is become aware of what your job is really all about. And stop playing the role of the victim who blames other people or events for the things that you don't like in your life and who acts as if your boss or your job or your company is responsible for whatever is going wrong.

Instead of that, what you want to do is exactly what you have been doing.

Create your game and give it a name.

Be sure that it is your game.

Set up your rules.

Be sure they are your rules.

Keep checking your internal experience of yourself, your body sensations, your emotional flow, your thoughts and your impressions and conclusions against your observations about the external reality of your job. And notice whenever something doesn't seem to fit correctly.

Do your homework and stay on top of whatever's wanted and needed so you can volunteer new ways to take care of it.

Keep looking for more and more ways to share yourself and make a contribution. And keep telling your boss how you are making it your job both to keep upgrading your own work and to see that he or she will always look good.

Participate. And let your participation make a difference in every life that touches your own.

Once you choose to make it all your game and to play it at a 100 percent level, who knows what you can accomplish and win.

Who knows?

You do.

Next up could be a big promotion in six months. Or your boss's job in 60 weeks. Or your own company in 60 months. Or chairman of the board in six years, maybe less.

It all starts with the raise you get in 60 days.

That's how it works.

Congratulate yourself. And enjoy it.

HOW TO GET MORE MONEY

- Go all-out in your Get A Raise Game. Don't hold anything back for the next time.
- Make and keep your game about getting a raise. Not about winning.
- Begin a new game immediately after you get your raise. Never stop playing.

Afterword and Acknowledgments

The only thing that's left to say about this book is that it works. You have my personal word about that.

My working experience both as a seeker of raises and as a giver of raises, provided much of the foundation. And the processes and exercises, particularly the idea of creating a game and enjoying how you play it out instead of trying and trying and trying to change an unworkable condition, come from my experiences as a successful independent creative consultant and freelance writer.

Creating your own game is the best and only way I know to consistently produce the results that make every area of your life challenging, rewarding and fun. That includes relationships, health and self-expression, as well as money. For me, it even includes getting clients and having books published.

As I said, it will work for you. And I invite you to make the most of it. And then, if you like, to write and tell me about it. I'm always looking for stories for future books, seminars and lectures.

Acknowledgments are definitely in order.

First, I want to thank each and every one of the department heads and managers who answered a questionnaire that I prepared and that Para Research incorporated into a mass mailing. Better than 10 percent of the people mailed responses. My personal acknowledgments to the following supervisors who signed their questionnaires and also to the twenty who chose to remain anonymous.

Ed Bauman	William Lovelace
Jeffrey H. Birk	Bernie Merlino
Ken Bruns	Roger Orlady
Jim Colombo	Bruce Pester
Eric Corbman	M. Lynn Rice
Jacqueline Proctor Daniels	Merle W. Richman, Jr.
James Delio	Rolla R. Ross
Joe Dresnok	Ed Savage
J.A. Emmendorfer	Kenneth C. Sassaman
Stephen J. Ferreira	Kevin R. Schopf
John H. Futter	John P. Schmidt
Betty Gouter	Robert A. Stevens
Gary Greenwood	David A. Stuntebeck
E.V. Guerra	Charles Sweeney
Dale L. Hughes	J. Carl Taylor
Lurton C. Keel, Jr.	Tim Tomlinson
Joan R. Kushner	Mark Wendleton
N. Lessard	Paul J. Zaboy

Next I want to thank Werner Erhard for coming up with the est Training and Seminar programs and for creating one of the finest playgrounds on the planet for discovering and expanding the power of your own intentions, the magic of keeping your word and the inherent ability within each of us to make a difference... Many of the abstractions in this book became clear to me through Werner's work.

My special, and I mean truly special, thanks are reserved for Jan Dragin for being and for becoming my partner in life during the creating of this book; for Jim McLellan, who supported me so completely with his friendship and his high-level managerial experiences; for Jennifer, for her astonishing and truly magic creative inspiration; and for Kitty, who relentlessly handled energy drains and boredom during the tedious mechanical typing of this manuscript and who died tragically and prematurely the day the book was completed.

Finally, I want to acknowledge each of the following for their contributions both to the content of this book and the content of my life while I was writing it. Each of them made my Writing Game for *Get A Raise in 60 Days* easier and more enjoyable.

Richard Abbadessa
Ted Abbadessa
Ron Abell
Charlene Afremow
Ina Ames
Helen Beyer
Priscilla Boettcher
Bob Brandt
Margie Brignac
Lorie Bruno
Amanda Burgoon
Tom Burgoon
Andrew Callen
Carolyn Coulter
Tom Cox
Paul Crimi
Budd Daniels
Joanna Daum
Roger Dillan
C. Jo Dorr
Jan Dragin
Carol Dubin
Werner Erhard

Robin Kappy
Edna Nightingale
   Kravette
Ellyn Kravette
Randolph Kravette
Sanford Kravette
Murray Kremer
Ken Krowne
Lana Kurtz
Shaun Levesque
Ted Long
Warren Manning
Jacque McLellan
Jim McLellan
Tom Michaelson
Frank David Molinski
Maggie Mountain
Joan Mullen
Judy Myers
Mark Myers
John O'Leary
Buryl Paine
Pep Peplinski

Dick Fewkes
Charles Giddings
Hazel Giddings
Rosanne Glickman
Jack Godler
Arthur Goldsmith, Jr.
Valerie Green
John Hall
George Hambly
Jan Hulian
Philip Johnson
Yalta Joslin
Leonard Kanzer
Stan Kaplan

Thelma Peplinskı
Andrew Petkun
Almeda F. Rood
Verne Schildhauer
Karol Senecal
Joe Sholes
Jim Sinatra
Jean Teich
Andrew Thornton
Jason Thornton
Norma Turner
Sally Williams
Rosian Zerner

GET A JOB
IN 60 SECONDS
by Steve Kravette

First impressions. Those are what get you a job or cause you to lose it. According to Steve Kravette, the person doing the hiring looks at you and your application at certain critical points for five seconds and forms an opinion. If you hold the interviewer's attention for the full five seconds, you advance to the next stage of the process. If not, your resume goes into the wastebasket. Once all those five second segments add up to 60 seconds, you've got the job you want.

Kravette's new book is brisk, outspoken and loud. He talked to the people who make the real decisions about hiring in some of the largest companies in the country. Combining this with his own experience in getting jobs and hiring people, he crystallized this unique approach to the most important task facing people today.

Get A Job In 60 Seconds takes the job hunter through all the major stages of getting a job. It tells the applicants what their mind-set should be and how they can beat the odds to keep the interviewer's attention focused on them and off the other candidates.

Complete and yet concise, this book is different from other books in the market in its basic approach. Employment manuals ask you to do complicated and time consuming exercises. *Get A Job In 60 Seconds* is not a manual. It is a direct ticket to employment. It relays its message in a boiled down fashion that gets the 60 second technique across. And the basic premise is reinforced at the end of each chapter as you see how to gain important seconds through a variety of graphics.

ISBN 0-914918-41-9
144 pages, 5¼"x 8", paper

$5.95

COMPLETE
MEDITATION

Steve Kravette

Complete Meditation presents a broad range of metaphysical concepts and
meditation techniques in the same direct, easy-to-assimilate style of the
author's best-selling *Complete Relaxation*. Personal experience is the teacher
and this unique book is your guide. The free, poetic format leads you
through a series of exercises that build on each other, starting with breathing
patterns, visualization exercises and a growing confidence that meditation is
easy and pleasurable. Graceful illustrations flow along with the text.

    Complete Meditation is for readers at all levels of experience. It makes
advanced metaphysics and esoteric practices accessible without years of study
of the literature, attachment to gurus or initiation into secret societies.
Everyone can meditate, everyone is psychic, and with only a little attention
everyone can bring oneself and one's circumstances into harmony.

    Experienced meditators will appreciate the more advanced techniques,
including more sophisticated breathing patterns, astral travel, past-life
regression, and much more. All readers will appreciate being shown how
ordinarily "boring" experiences are really illuminating gateways into the
complete meditation experience. Whether you do all the exercises or not, just
reading this book is a pleasure.

    Complete meditation can happen anywhere, any time, in thousands of
different ways. A candle flame, a daydream, music, sex, a glint of light on
your ring. In virtually any circumstances. *Complete Meditation* shows you
how.

ISBN 0-914918-28-1
309 pages, 6½" x 9¼", paper, $9.95

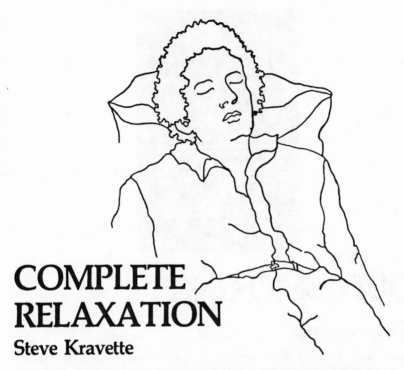

COMPLETE RELAXATION

Steve Kravette

Complete Relaxation is unique in its field because, unlike most relaxation books, it takes a completely relaxed approach to its subject. You will find a series of poetic explorations interspersed with text and beautifully drawn illustrations designed to put you in closer touch with yourself and the people around you. *Complete Relaxation* is written for all of you: your body, your mind, your emotions, your spirituality, your sexuality—the whole person you are and are meant to be.

As you read this book, you will begin to feel yourself entering a way of life more completely relaxed than you ever thought possible. Reviewer Ben Reuven stated in the *Los Angeles Times*, "*Complete Relaxation* came along at just the right time—I read it, tried it; it works."

Some of the many areas that the author touches upon are: becoming aware, instant relaxation, stretching, hatha yoga, Arica, bioenergetics, Tai chi, dancing, and the Relaxation Reflex.

Mantras, meditating, emotional relaxation, holding back and letting go, learning to accept yourself, business relaxation, driving relaxation.

Family relaxation, nutritional relaxation, spiritual relaxation, sensual relaxation, massage and sexual relaxation. *Complete Relaxation* is a book the world has been tensely, nervously, anxiously waiting for. Here it is. Read it and relax.

ISBN 0-914918-14-1
320 pages, 6½" x 9¼", paper, $9.95

Proven techniques to help you quit forever

Smoking

Most books simply entertain. Rarely does a book come along that can save lives. **Quit Smoking** is one of those books. It is the definitive book on all aspects of smoking, filled with good news and good suggestions for cigarette smokers who want to live.

Quit Smoking offers an excellent overview of the problems of smoking and shows a promise, the light at the end of the tunnel, for smokers interested in kicking their habit. It covers the programs, the therapies, the statistics, the problem itself.

As a writer can best describe a problem he has known, Curtis Casewit describes his own cigarette addiction and his successful cure. And he has not relapsed in 10 years! **Quit Smoking** tells it like it is and tells it all. This book is for smokers, families of smokers and non-smokers. —Sidney L. Werkman, M.D.

CURTIS CASEWIT

QUIT SMOKING

Curtis Casewit

Author Curtis Casewit calls smoking the new social stigma. Never before has there been such a clear, concise and complete guide to the dangers of smoking and how to stop. *Quit Smoking* is sure to convince any smoker that he or she ought to stop, and best of all, it gives them the means.

Quit Smoking presents over 40 techniques which can help anyone stop smoking forever. Casewit surveys cessation programs all over the world to present as complete a guide on how to stop smoking as possible. Casewit's aim is twofold: first, he presents a number of individual stop smoking programs for the person who wants to stop on his or her own. Second, he reviews the major group cessation programs for those who need the support of others working to conquer the same problem.

From self-hypnosis to the Seventh Day Adventist Five Day Stop Smoking Plan, Casewit has done a truly major survey of the most successful methods used to stop smoking. *Quit Smoking* is full of charts on the effects of smoking and contains a detailed description of how the powerful tobacco lobby works for the interest of the cigarette industry in the United States.

Curtis Casewit is a former smoker and author of over 20 books. He began collecting information for this book when he quit his two pack a day habit. He was successful, and millions of other smokers can discover their own successful methods in *Quit Smoking*.

Introduction by Sidney L. Werkman, M.D.
ISBN 0-914918-44-3
144 pages, paper

$7.95

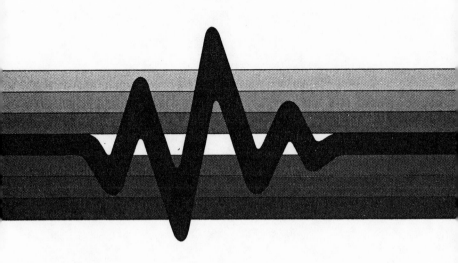

GOOD NIGHT

Norman Ford

Insomnia can be overcome naturally, without the use of drugs. *Good Night* is the book that tells you all about sleeping, insomnia and learning how to sleep again. Professional health writer Norman Ford has studied the insomnia problem and synthesized the work being done to fight it.

Recent studies indicate that almost 20 percent of Americans suffers from one or more of the six major forms of insomnia. This all too common problem is making us irritable and adding more stress to our already stressful world. Insomnia can be overcome by first understanding what it is that keeps us awake and then implementing the proper steps to help us sleep well again. After investivating the causes of sleeplessness, *Good Night* tells insomniacs what not to do and presents several programs which will assure the best possible night's sleep.

This is a comprehensive book that tells the reader how to achieve a nealthier lifestyle through better sleep. This book will tell you what good sleep is, why drugs and medical techniques probably won't help you sleep and what you can do to sleep better naturally. *Good Night* is the one personal investment that is guaranteed to make you sleep better at night.

ISBN 0-914918-47-8
208 pages, paper

$8.95